interchange

THIRD EDITION

Jack C. Richards
with Jonathan Hull and Susan Proctor

STUDENT'S BOOK

2

CAMBRIDGE UNIVERSITY PRESS
Cambridge, New York, Melbourne, Madrid, Cape Town, Singapore, São Paulo

Cambridge University Press
40 West 20th Street, New York, NY 10011–4211, USA

www.cambridge.org
Information on this title: www.cambridge.org/9780521601948

First published 2005
11th printing 2006

Interchange Third Edition Student's Book 2 has been developed from *New Interchange*
Student's Book 2, first published by Cambridge University Press in 1997.

Printed in Hong Kong, China, by Golden Cup Printing Company Limited

A catalog record for this publication is available from the British Library

ISBN-13 978-0-521-60194-8 student's book
ISBN-10 0-521-60194-0 student's book

Art direction, book design, photo research, and layout services: Adventure House, NYC
Audio production: Richard LePage & Associates

To the student

Welcome to *Interchange Third Edition*! This revised edition of *New Interchange* gives you many more opportunities to learn and practice English. We are confident this book will help you improve your English! The course combines topics, functions, and grammar. You will learn the four skills of listening, speaking, reading, and writing, in addition to vocabulary and pronunciation.

Each book has 16 units divided into sections, and each section has its own purpose. The **Snapshot** usually introduces the unit's topic with real-world information. The **Word Power** presents new vocabulary. **Perspectives** is a new section that uses people's opinions and experiences about a topic to present new grammar. The **Conversation** is a natural, fun dialog that also introduces new grammar. You then see and practice this language in the **Grammar Focus**. The **Pronunciation** exercises help you sound like a native speaker.

In the **Listening** section you hear people speaking in many different contexts. You talk in pairs, in groups, or as a class with the many **Speaking** activities. In the **Interchange activities** you talk even more freely about yourself. These fun activities let you share your own ideas and opinions. In the **Writing** section you write about yourself and your classmates. Finally, at the end of each unit, you read about and further discuss the unit's topic in the **Reading** section.

Frequent **Progress checks** let you check your own development. In these self-assessment exercises *you* decide what material you need to review.

The **Self-study Audio CD** contains the conversations from the unit for extra listening practice. Your CD also has a section with new, original audio material. You can use this in class, in a lab, or at home with the Self-study exercises at the back of this book.

We think you'll enjoy using this book and hope you become better, more confident learners of English. Good luck!

Jack C. Richards
Jonathan Hull
Susan Proctor

Authors' acknowledgments

A great number of people contributed to the development of *Interchange Third Edition*. Particular thanks are owed to the following:

The **reviewers** using *New Interchange* in the following schools and institutes – their insights and suggestions have helped define the content and format of the third edition: Gino Pumadera, **American School**, Guayaquil, Ecuador; Don Ahn, **APEX**, Seoul, Korea; Linda Martinez, **Canada College**, Redwood City, California, USA; Rosa Maria Valencia Rodriguez, **CEMARC**, Mexico City, Mexico; Wendel Mendes Dantas, **Central Universitária**, São Paulo, Brazil; Lee Altschuler, **Cheng Kung University**, Tainan, Taiwan; Chun Mao Le, **Cheng Siu Institute of Technology**, Kaohsiung, Taiwan; Selma Alfonso, **Colégio Arquidiocesano**, São Paulo, Brazil; Daniel de Mello Ferraz, **Colégio Camargo Aranha**, São Paulo, Brazil; Paula dos Santos Dames, **Colegio Militar do Rio de Janeiro**, Rio de Janeiro, Brazil; Elizabeth Ortiz, **COPOL-COPEI**, Guayaquil, Ecuador; Alexandre de Oliveira, **First Idiomas**, São Paulo, Brazil; João Franco Júnior, **2B Idiomas**, São Paulo, Brazil; Jo Ellen Kaiser and David Martin, **Fort Lauderdale High School**, Fort Lauderdale, Florida, USA; Azusa Okada, **Hiroshima Shudo University**, Hiroshima, Japan; Sandra Herrera and Rosario Valdiria, **INACAP**, Santiago, Chile; Samara Camilo Tome Costa, **Instituto Brasil-Estados Unidos**, Rio de Janeiro, Brazil; Eric Hamilton, **Instituto Chileno Norteamericano de Cultura**, Santiago, Chile; **ICNA**, Santiago, Chile; Pedro Benites, Carolina Chenett, Elena Montero Hurtado, Patricia Nieto, and Antonio Rios, **Instituto Cultural Peruano Norteamericano (ICPNA)**, Lima, Peru; Vanclei Nascimento, **Instituto Pentágono**, São Paulo, Brazil; Michael T. Thornton, **Interactive College of Technology**, Chamblee, Georgia, USA; Norma Aguilera Celis, **IPN ESCA Santo Tomas**, Mexico City, Mexico; Lewis Barksdale, **Kanazawa Institute of Technology**, Ishikawa, Japan; Clare St. Lawrence, Gill Christie, and Sandra Forrester, **Key Language Services**, Quito, Ecuador; Érik Mesquita, **King's Cross**, São Paulo, Brazil; Robert S. Dobie, **Kojen English Language Schools**, Taipei, Taiwan; Shoko Miyagi, **Madison Area Technical College**, Madison, Wisconsin, USA; Atsuko K. Yamazaki, **Institute of Technologists**, Saitama, Japan; teachers and students at **Institute of Technologists**, Saitama, Japan; Gregory Hadley, **Niigata University of International and Information Studies**, Niigata, Japan; Tony Brewer and Frank Claypool, **Osaka College of Foreign Languages and International Business**, Osaka, Japan; Chris Kerr, **Osaka University of Economics and Law**, Osaka, Japan; Angela Suzete Zumpano, **Personal Language Center**, São Paulo, Brazil; Simon Banha Jr. and Tomas S. Martins, **Phil Young's English School**, Curitiba, Brazil; Mehran Sabet and Bob Diem, **Seigakuin University**, Saitama, Japan; Lily Beam, **Shie Jen University**, Kaohsiung, Taiwan; Ray Sullivan, **Shibuya Kyoiku Gakuen Makuhari Senior and Junior High School**, Chiba, Japan; Robert Gee, **Sugiyama Jogakuen University**, Nagoya, Japan; Arthur Tu, **Taipei YMCA**, Taipei, Taiwan; Hiroko Nishikage, Alan Hawk, Peter Riley, and Peter Anyon, **Taisho University**, Tokyo, Japan; Vera Berk, **Talkative Idiomas**, São Paulo, Brazil; Patrick D. McCoy, **Toyo University**, Saitama, Japan; Kathleen Krokar and Ellen D. Sellergren, **Truman College**, Chicago, Illinois, USA; Gabriela Cortes Sanchez, **UAM-A**, Mexico City, Mexico; Marco A. Mora Piedra, **Universidad de Costa Rica**, San Jose, Costa Rica; Janette Carvalhinho de Oliveira, **Universidade Federal do Espirito Santo**, Vitoria, Brazil; Belem Saint Martin Lozada, **Universidad ISEC**, Colegio del Valle, Mexico City, Mexico; Robert Sanchez Flores, **Universidad Nacional Autonoma de Mexico**, Centro de Lenguas Campus Aragon, Mexico City, Mexico; Bertha Chela de Rodriguez, **Universidad Simòn Bolìvar**, Caracas, Venezuela; Marilyn Johnson, **Washoe High School**, Reno, Nevada, USA; Monika Soens, **Yen Ping Senior High School**, Taipei, Taiwan; Kim Yoon Gyong, **Yonsei University**, Seoul, Korea; and Tania Borges Lobao, **York Language Institute**, Rio de Janeiro, Brazil.

The **editorial** and **production** team:
David Bohlke, Jeff Chen, Yuri Hara, Pam Harris, Paul Heacock, Louisa Hellegers, Lise R. Minovitz, Pat Nelson, Bill Paulk, Danielle Power, Mary Sandre, Tami Savir, Kayo Taguchi, Louisa van Houten, Mary Vaughn, Jennifer Wilkin, and Dorothy Zemach.

And Cambridge University Press **staff** and **advisors**:
Jim Anderson, Angela Andrade, Mary Louise Baez, Carlos Barbisan, Kathleen Corley, Kate Cory-Wright, Elizabeth Fuzikava, Steve Golden, Cecilia Gomez, Heather Gray, Bob Hands, Pauline Ireland, Ken Kingery, Gareth Knight, Nigel McQuitty, João Madureira, Andy Martin, Alejandro Martinez, Carine Mitchell, Mark O'Neill, Tom Price, Dan Schulte, Catherine Shih, Howard Siegelman, Ivan Sorrentino, Alcione Tavares, Koen Van Landeghem, and Ellen Zlotnick.

CLASSROOM LANGUAGE Working together

Plan of Book 2

Titles/Topics	Speaking	Grammar
UNIT 1 PAGES 2-7		
A time to remember People; childhood; memories	Introducing yourself; talking about yourself; exchanging personal information; remembering your childhood; asking about someone's childhood	Past tense; *used to* for habitual actions
UNIT 2 PAGES 8-13		
Caught in the rush Transportation; transportation problems; city services	Talking about transportation and transportation problems; evaluating city services; asking for and giving information	Adverbs of quantity with count and noncount nouns: *too many, too much, fewer, less, more, not enough*; indirect questions from Wh-questions
PROGRESS CHECK PAGES 14-15		
UNIT 3 PAGES 16-21		
Time for a change! Houses and apartments; lifestyle changes; wishes	Describing positive and negative features; making comparisons; talking about lifestyle changes; expressing wishes	Evaluations and comparisons with adjectives: *not . . . enough, too, (not) as . . . as*; evaluations and comparisons with nouns: *not enough . . . , too much/many, . . . , (not) as much/many . . . as; wish*
UNIT 4 PAGES 22-27		
I've never heard of that! Food; recipes; instructions; cooking methods	Talking about food; expressing likes and dislikes; describing a favorite snack; giving instructions	Simple past vs. present perfect; sequence adverbs: *first, then, next, after that, finally*
PROGRESS CHECK PAGES 28-29		
UNIT 5 PAGES 30-35		
Going places Travel; vacations; plans	Describing vacation plans; giving travel advice; planning a vacation	Future with *be going to* and *will*; modals for necessity and suggestion: *must, need to, (don't) have to, better, ought to, should (not)*
UNIT 6 PAGES 36-41		
OK. No problem! Complaints; household chores; requests; excuses; apologies	Making requests; accepting and refusing requests; complaining; apologizing; giving excuses	Two-part verbs; *will* for responding to requests; requests with modals and *Would you mind . . . ?*
PROGRESS CHECK PAGES 42-43		
UNIT 7 PAGES 44-49		
What's this for? Technology; instructions	Describing technology; giving instructions; giving suggestions	Infinitives and gerunds for uses and purposes; imperatives and infinitives for giving suggestions
UNIT 8 PAGES 50-55		
Let's celebrate! Holidays; festivals; customs; celebrations	Describing holidays, festivals, customs, and special events	Relative clauses of time; adverbial clauses of time: *when, after, before*
PROGRESS CHECK PAGES 56-57		

Pronunciation/Listening	Writing/Reading	Interchange Activity
Reduced form of *used to* Listening to people talk about their past *Self-study*: Listening to people discuss their favorite childhood memories	Writing a paragraph about your childhood "Nicole Kidman: New Hollywood Royalty": Reading about an actress's career	"Class profile": Finding out about a classmate's childhood
Syllable stress Listening to a description of a transportation system *Self-study*: Listening to people ask for information	Writing a letter to the editor "New Ways of Getting Around": Reading about new transportation inventions	"Tourism campaign": Suggesting ways to attract tourists to a city
Unpronounced vowels Listening to people talk about capsule hotels *Self-study*: Listening to people ask and answer questions about apartments for rent	Writing an e-mail describing an apartment "Break Those Bad Habits": Reading about ways to end bad habits	"Wishful thinking": Finding out about classmate's wishes
Consonant clusters Listening to descriptions of foods *Self-study*: Listening to people talk about food	Writing a recipe "Food and Mood": Reading about how food affects the way we feel	"Risky business": Collecting personal information from classmates
Linked sounds with /w/ and /y/ Listening to travel advice *Self-study*: Listening to people discuss vacation plans	Writing travel suggestions "Getting Away From It All": Reading tips from an expert backpacker	"Fun vacations": Deciding on a trip
Stress in two-part verbs Listening to results of a survey *Self-study*: Listening to people make requests	Writing a set of guidelines "Neighbor vs. Neighbor": Reading about ways to deal with neighbors	"That's no excuse!": Apologizing and making excuses
Syllable stress Listening to a radio program; listening to people give advice *Self-study*: Listening to people discuss computers	Writing a note giving instructions "A Day in Your Life – In the Year 2020": Reading about life in the future	"Talk radio": Giving advice to classmates
Stress and rhythm Listening to a description of Carnaval *Self-study*: Listening to someone talk about Halloween	Writing a travel guide "Unique Customs": Reading about holidays and unusual customs	"Once in a blue moon": Finding out how classmates celebrate special events

Titles/Topics	Speaking	Grammar

1 A time to remember

1 SNAPSHOT

Getting to Know You

Many people use the Internet to meet people. Here is some typical information found in online personal ads.

Tell us about yourself!

Ted

Background
Born: Dallas
Grew up: Los Angeles

Professional information
Education: college degree
Occupation: computer specialist

Interests and hobbies
I love to be outdoors. I enjoy skiing
and swimming. And I'm a good cook.

Background
Born: Buenos Aires
Grew up: Los Angeles

Professional information
Education: high school diploma
Occupation: college student

Interests and hobbies
I like to go to the movies and take long
walks. And I'm learning to in-line skate!

Ana

Source: *http://personals.yahoo.com*

Do you think Ana and Ted could be friends?
Do people in your country use personal ads? How else can people meet?
Create your own personal profile and compare it with a partner.
  How are you the same? different?

2 CONVERSATION *Where did you learn to skate?*

A ▶ Listen and practice.

Ted: Oh, I'm really sorry. Are you OK?
Ana: I'm fine. But I'm not very good at this.
Ted: Neither am I. . . . Say, are you from South America?
Ana: Yes, I am, originally. I was born in Argentina.
Ted: Did you grow up there?
Ana: Yes, I did, but my family moved here
    ten years ago, when I was in junior high school.
Ted: And where did you learn to skate?
Ana: Here in the park. This is only my third time.
Ted: Well, it's my *first* time. Can you give me some lessons?
Ana: Sure. Just follow me.
Ted: By the way, my name is Ted.
Ana: And I'm Ana. Nice to meet you.

B ▶ Listen to the rest of the conversation. What are
two more things you learn about Ted?

3 GRAMMAR FOCUS

Past tense ▶

Where **were** you born?
   I **was** born in Argentina.

Were you born in Buenos Aires?
   Yes, I **was**.
   No, I **wasn't**. I **was** born in Córdoba.

When **did** you **move** to Los Angeles?
   I **moved** here ten years ago. I **didn't speak** English.

Did you **take** English classes in Argentina?
   Yes, I **did**. I **took** classes for a year.
   No, I **didn't**. My aunt **taught** me at home.

A Complete these conversations. Then practice with a partner.

1. A: Could you tell me a little about yourself?
    Where ………… you born?
  B: I ………… born in Korea.
  A: ………… you grow up there?
  B: No, I ………… . I ………… up in Canada.

2. A: Where ………… you go to high school?
  B: I ………… to high school in Ecuador.
  A: And when ………… you graduate?
  B: I ………… last year. Now I work as a salesperson.

3. A: ………… you have a favorite teacher when
    you ………… a child?
  B: Yes, I ………… . I ………… an excellent
    teacher named Mr. Woods.
  A: What ………… he teach?
  B: He ………… English.

B *Pair work* Take turns asking the questions in part A. Give your own information when answering.

4 LISTENING Life as an immigrant

A ▶ Listen to interviews with two immigrants to the United States. Where are they from?

B ▶ Listen again and complete the chart.

	Yu Hong	Ajay
1. When did he/she move to the United States?	………………………	………………………
2. What is difficult about being an immigrant?	………………………	………………………
3. What does he/she miss the most?	………………………	………………………

5 SPEAKING Tell me about yourself.

A *Pair work* Check (✓) six questions below. Then interview a classmate you don't know very well.

☐ Where did you go to elementary school?
☐ Were you a good student in elementary school?
☐ What were your best subjects?
☐ What subjects didn't you like?
☐ When did you first study English?

☐ What other languages can you speak?
☐ Do you have a big family?
☐ Did you enjoy your childhood?
☐ Who was your hero when you were a child?
☐ Did you ever have a part-time job?

B *Group work* Tell the group what you learned about your partner. Then answer any questions.

A: Carlos went to elementary school in Mexico City.
B: Pam first studied English when she was 10.
C: Really? Where did she study English?

useful expressions
Really? Me, too! Wow! What was it like? Can you tell us more?

6 WORD POWER

A Complete the word map. Add two more words to each category. Then compare with a partner.

✓ beach
  bicycle
  cat
  collect comic books
  paint
  play chess
  rabbit
  scrapbook
  snake
  soccer ball
  summer camp
  tree house

Pets

Hobbies

Childhood memories

Places
beach

Possessions

B *Pair work* Choose three words from the word map and use them to describe some of your childhood memories.

A: I played chess when I was in elementary school.
B: How well did you play?
A: I was pretty good, actually. I won several competitions.

7 PERSPECTIVES *How have you changed?*

A  Listen to these statements about changes. Check (✓) those that are true about you.

- [ ] 1. "When I was a kid, I used to be very messy, but now I'm very neat."
- [ ] 2. "I used to have a lot of hobbies, but now I don't have any free time."
- [ ] 3. "I didn't use to collect anything, but now I do."
- [ ] 4. "I used to be really into fashion, but these days I'm not interested anymore."
- [ ] 5. "I never used to play sports, but now I like to keep fit."
- [ ] 6. "I never used to worry about money, but now I do."
- [ ] 7. "I didn't use to follow politics, but now I read the newspaper every day."
- [ ] 8. "When I was younger, I used to care a lot about my appearance. Now, I'm too busy to care how I look."

B *Pair work* Look at the statements again. Which changes are positive? Which are negative?

"I think the first one is a positive change. It's good to be neat."

8 GRAMMAR FOCUS

Used to ▶

Used to refers to something that you regularly did in the past but don't do anymore.

I **used to** be very messy, but now I'm very neat.
Did you **use to** collect things?
    Yes, I **used to** collect comic books.
    No, I **didn't use to** collect anything, but now I collect art.
What sports **did** you **use to** play?
    I **never used to** play sports, but now I play tennis.

A Complete these sentences. Then compare with a partner.

1. In elementary school, I used to . . .
2. I used to be . . . , but I'm not anymore.
3. When I was a kid, I used to play . . .
4. I didn't use to . . .
5. After school, my best friend and I used to . . .
6. My parents never used to . . .

B *Pair work* How have you changed these things? Write five more sentences about yourself using *used to*.

your hairstyle   the way you dress   your hobbies and interests

"I used to wear my hair much longer. Now I wear it short."

9 PRONUNCIATION Used to

A ▶ Listen and practice. Notice that the pronunciation of **used to** and **use to** is the same.

When I was a child, I **used to** play the trumpet.
    I **used to** have a nickname.
    I didn't **use to** have a bicycle.
    I didn't **use to** study very hard at school.

B *Pair work* Practice the sentences you wrote in Exercise 8 again. Pay attention to the pronunciation of **used to** and **use to**.

10 SPEAKING Memories

A *Pair work* Add three questions to this list. Then take turns asking and answering the questions.

1. What's your favorite childhood memory?
2. What kinds of sports or games did you use to play when you were younger?
3. Did you use to have a nickname?
4. Where did you use to spend your vacations?
5. How has your taste in music changed?
6. ....
7. ....
8. ....

B *Class activity* Tell the class two interesting things about your partner.

11 WRITING About yourself

A Write a paragraph about things you used to do as a child. Use some of your ideas from Exercise 10. Just for fun, include one false statement.

> When I was four years old, my family moved to Australia. We had an old two-story house and a big yard. My older brother and I used to play lots of games together. In the summer, my favorite outdoor game was . . .

B *Group work* Share your paragraphs and answer any questions. Can you find the false statements?

12 INTERCHANGE 1 Class profile

Find out more about your classmates. Go to Interchange 1 at the back of the book.

Nicole Kidman: New Hollywood Royalty

Scan the article. Where was Nicole Kidman born? Where was she married? When did she win an Academy Award?

Actress Nicole Kidman was born in Honolulu, Hawaii, in 1967. Her father, an Australian, was a student in Hawaii at the time. When she was 4, the family returned to Australia, and Kidman grew up in a suburb of Sydney.

Kidman became interested in acting early on. Her first experience came when she was 6 years old and she played a sheep in her school's Christmas pageant. She trained in drama and dance through her teen years. She got a couple of TV parts before she made her breakthrough: In 1985, the Australian Film Institute named her Actress of the Year for her role in the TV miniseries *Vietnam*. She was only 17.

In 1989, Kidman appeared in the creepy thriller *Dead Calm*. This performance earned her the lead role in her first American movie, *Days of Thunder*. Her costar was Tom Cruise. Following a whirlwind romance, Kidman and Cruise were married in Colorado on Christmas Eve, 1990.

During the marriage, Kidman's career continued to grow. She and Cruise adopted two children, and they worked hard to balance their careers and family life.

One of the most fascinating actresses of our time

Unfortunately, the marriage didn't last. Kidman and Cruise divorced in 2001. After the divorce, Kidman threw herself into her work. She starred in a number of high-profile movies, including the musical *Moulin Rouge*. Then, in 2003, she won both an Academy Award and a Golden Globe for her role as Virginia Woolf in the film *The Hours*.

And what does she think of her fame? "It's a fleeting moment," she has said. "How long will it last? Who knows? But it's here and it's now."

A Read the article. Find the words in *italics* in the article. Then circle the meaning of each word or phrase.

1. When you make a *breakthrough*, you experience a sudden **advance** / **accident**.
2. When something is *creepy*, it gives you a feeling of **joy and excitement** / **fear and disgust**.
3. A *whirlwind* describes something that happens **slowly** / **quickly**.
4. When Kidman *threw herself into* her work, she **worked very hard** / **stopped working**.
5. When something is *fleeting*, it lasts a **short** / **long** time.

B Number these sentences from 1 (first event) to 10 (last event).

.... a. She divorced Tom Cruise.
.... b. She had her first acting experience.
.... c. She won an Academy Award.
.... d. She moved to Australia.
.... e. She made her first American movie.
.... f. She won her first award.
.... g. She adopted two children.
...*1*... h. She was born in Hawaii.
.... i. She studied drama and dance.
.... j. She married Tom Cruise.

C *Pair work* Who is your favorite actor or actress? What interesting details do you know about his or her life and career?

2 Caught in the rush

1 WORD POWER Compound nouns

A Match the words in columns A and B to make compound nouns.
(More than one answer may be possible.)

subway + station = subway station

A	B
bicycle	garage
bus	jam
news	lane
parking	light
street	space
subway	stand
taxi	station
traffic	stop
train	system

a taxi stand

a bicycle lane

B *Pair work* Which of these things can you find where you live?

A: There is a bus system here.
B: Yes. There are also a lot of traffic jams.

2 PERSPECTIVES Transportation services

A ▶ Listen to these comments about transportation services.

"I think there are too many cars on the road. All the cars, taxis, and buses make it really dangerous for bicycles. There is too much traffic!"

"What about the buses? They are old, slow, and cause too much pollution. I think there should be less pollution in the city."

"There should be fewer cars, but I think that the biggest problem is parking. There just isn't enough parking."

B *Pair work* Look at the comments again. Which statements do you agree with?

3 GRAMMAR FOCUS

Adverbs of quantity ▷

With count nouns	With noncount nouns
There are **too many** cars.	There is **too much** traffic.
There should be **fewer** cars.	There should be **less** pollution.
We need **more** subway lines.	We need **more** public transportation.
There are**n't enough** buses.	There is**n't enough** parking.

A Complete these statements about transportation problems. Then compare with a partner. (More than one answer may be possible.)

1. There are .... police officers.
2. There should be .... cars in the city.
3. There is .... public transportation.
4. The government needs to build .... highways.
5. There should be .... noise.
6. We should have .... public parking garages.
7. There is .... air pollution in the city.
8. There are .... cars parked on the streets.

B *Group work* Write sentences about the city or town you are living in. Then compare with others.

1. The city should provide more . . .
2. We have too many . . .
3. There's too much . . .
4. There isn't enough . . .
5. There should be fewer . . .
6. We don't have enough . . .
7. There should be less . . .
8. We need more . . .

4 LISTENING *Singapore solves it.*

A ▷ Listen to someone talk about how Singapore has tried to solve its traffic problems. Check (✓) True or False for each statement.

	True	False
1. Motorists are never allowed to drive into the business district.	☐	☐
2. People need a special certificate to buy a car.	☐	☐
3. Cars cost more than in the United States or Canada.	☐	☐
4. Public transportation still needs to be improved.	☐	☐

B ▷ Listen again. For the false statements, write the correct information.

C *Class activity* Could the solutions adopted in Singapore work in your city or town? Why or why not?

5 DISCUSSION *You be the judge!*

A *Group work* Which of these transportation services are available in your city or town? Discuss what is good and bad about each one.

.... taxi service   .... the subway system   .... facilities for pedestrians
.... the bus system   .... the train system   .... parking

B *Group work* How would you rate the transportation services where you live? Give each item a rating from 1 to 5.

5 = excellent   4 = good   3 = average   2 = needs improvement   1 = terrible

A: I'd give the taxi service a rating of 4. There are enough taxis, but there are too many bad drivers.
B: I think a rating of 4 is too high. There should be more taxi stands and . . .

6 WRITING *A letter to the editor*

A Read this letter to a newspaper editor about traffic problems in the city.

B Use your statements from Exercise 3 and any new ideas to write a letter to your local newspaper.

C *Pair work* Take turns reading your letters. Give your partner suggestions for revision.

> To whom it may concern:
>
> There's too much traffic in this city, and it's getting worse! A few years ago, it took me ten minutes to get downtown. Now it takes more than *thirty* minutes during the rush hour! Here are my suggestions to solve some of our traffic problems. First of all, there should be more subway lines. I think people want to use public transportation, but we need more . . .

7 SNAPSHOT

Common Questions
Asked by Visitors to a City

☐ How much do cabs cost?
☐ Where can I get a map?
☐ Where can I rent a cell phone?
☐ Where can I walk my dog?
☐ Which hotel is closest to the airport?

☐ Where is the best place to meet friends?
☐ What's an inexpensive way to sightsee?
☐ Where should I go shopping?
☐ What are some interesting stores?
☐ What museums should I see?

Sources: *www.choosechicago.com*; *www.orlandoairports.net*

Check (✓) the questions you can answer about your city.
What other questions could a visitor ask about your city?
Talk to your classmates. Find answers to the questions you didn't check.

CONVERSATION *Could you tell me . . . ?*

A ▶ Listen and practice.

Erica: Excuse me. Could you tell me where the bank is?
Clerk: There's one upstairs, across from the duty-free shop.
Erica: Do you know what time it opens?
Clerk: It should be open now. It opens at 8:00 A.M.
Erica: Oh, good. And can you tell me how often the buses leave for the city?
Clerk: You need to check at the transportation counter. It's right down the hall.
Erica: OK. And just one more thing. Do you know where the rest rooms are?
Clerk: Right behind you. Do you see where that sign is?
Erica: Oh. Thanks a lot.

AIRPORT INFORMATION

B ▶ Listen to the rest of the conversation.
Check (✓) the information that Erica asks for.

☐ the cost of a taxi to the city   ☐ the cost of a bus to the city
☐ the location of the taxi stand   ☐ the location of a restaurant

GRAMMAR FOCUS

Indirect questions from Wh-questions ▷

Wh-questions with be	*Indirect questions*
Where is the bank?	Could you tell me **where the bank is**?
Where are the rest rooms?	Do you know **where the rest rooms are**?

Wh-questions with do *or* did	*Indirect questions*
How often do the buses leave?	Can you tell me **how often the buses leave**?
What time does the bank open?	Do you know **what time the bank opens**?
When did Flight 566 arrive?	Do you know **when Flight 566 arrived**?

A Write indirect questions using these Wh-questions.
Then compare with a partner.

1. How much does a newspaper cost?
2. Where is the nearest cash machine?
3. What time do the banks open?
4. How often do the buses come?
5. Where can you get a good meal?
6. How late do the nightclubs stay open?
7. How early do the trains run?
8. What is the best hotel in the area?

B *Pair work* Take turns asking the questions you wrote in part A.
Give your own information when answering.

"Do you know how much a newspaper costs?"

10 PRONUNCIATION Syllable stress

A ▶ Listen and practice. Notice which syllable has the main stress in these two-syllable words.

● ○	○ ●
subway	garage
traffic	police

B ▶ Listen to the stress in these words. Write them in the correct column. Then compare with a partner.

		● ○	○ ●
buses	improve	....	....
newsstand	provide	....	....
hotel	public	....	....
taxis	machine	....	....

11 SPEAKING What do you know?

A Complete the chart with indirect questions.

	Name:	Name: ....
1. Where is the tourist information center? "*Can you tell me where* .... ?"	....	....
2. What time do the stores close? " .... ?"	....	....
3. Where is the nearest hospital? " .... ?"	....	....
4. How much does a taxi to the airport cost? " .... ?"	....	....
5. Where can I find a good shopping mall? " .... ?"	....	....
6. Where is the nearest drugstore? " .... ?"	....	....
7. What is a good place for families with children? " .... ?"	....	....

B *Group work* Use the indirect questions in the chart to interview two classmates about the city or town where you live. Take notes.

A: Can you tell me where the tourist information center is?
B: I'm not really sure, but I think . . .

C *Class activity* Share your answers with the class. Who knows the most about your city or town?

12 INTERCHANGE 2 Tourism campaign

Discuss ways to attract tourists to a city. Go to Interchange 2 at the back of the book.

NEW WAYS OF *Getting Around*

Look at the pictures and skim the article. Then write the name of the invention below each picture.

Outrider   PowerSki Jetboard   TrikkeScooter   Wheelman

Here are some of the best new inventions for getting around on land and sea.

On land

If you love to take risks when you travel, this is for you: the **Wheelman**. The design is simple: two wheels and a motor. You put your feet in the wheels. It's very similar to skateboarding or surfing. You use your weight to steer and control the speed with a ball you hold in your hand.

Why use two wheels when you can use three? The **Trikke Scooter** looks a little silly, but it's serious transportation. The three wheels make it very stable. And because it's made of aluminum, it's very light. It moves by turning back and forth – just like skiing on the street.

On sea

If you're the kind of person who enjoys being out at sea, but suffers from motion sickness, the **OutRider** will interest you. The boat is attached to a strange-looking ski, allowing it to move smoothly over the water, even at high speeds. It's perfect for those who refuse to give up their love of boating over an upset stomach.

Do you ever feel like surfing when the sea is too flat? Then you need the **PowerSki Jetboard**, a board that makes its own waves. This creation brings together the ease of waterskiing and the freedom of surfing. A former pro surfer designed the lightweight engine to be able to stir up even the calmest water.

A Read the article. Where do you think it is from? Check (✓) the correct answer.

☐ an instruction manual   ☐ a catalog   ☑ a newsmagazine   ☐ an encyclopedia

B Answer these questions.

1. Which inventions have motors? ....
2. Where do you put your feet in the Wheelman? ....
3. How do you steer the Wheelman? ....
4. What makes the Trikke Scooter stable? ....
5. How does the Trikke Scooter move? ....
6. What makes the OutRider move smoothly on the water? ....
7. What two sports does the PowerSki Jetboard combine? ....
8. Who designed the engine for the PowerSki Jetboard? ....

C *Pair work* Which of the above inventions is the most useful? the least useful? Would you like to try any of them?

Units 1-2 Progress check

SELF-ASSESSMENT

How well can you do these things? Check (✓) the boxes.

I can	Very well	OK	A little
Listen to and understand the past tense and *used to* (Ex. 1)	☐	☐	☐
Ask and answer questions using the past tense and *used to* (Ex. 1, 2)	☐	☐	☐
Talk about city services using adverbs of quantity (Ex. 3)	☐	☐	☐
Ask for and give information using indirect questions (Ex. 4)	☐	☐	☐

1 LISTENING Celebrity interview

A ▶ Listen to an interview with Jeri, a fashion model. Answer the questions.

1. Where did she grow up? ....
2. What did she want to do when she grew up? ....
3. Did she have a hobby? ....
4. Did she have a favorite game? ....
5. What was her favorite place? ....

B *Pair work* Use the questions in part A to interview a partner about his or her childhood. Ask additional questions to get more information.

2 DISCUSSION How times have changed!

A *Pair work* Talk about how life in your country has changed in the last 50 years. Ask questions like these:

How big were families 50 years ago?
What kinds of homes did people live in?
How did people use to dress?
How were schools different?
What kinds of jobs did men have? women?
How much did people use to earn?

B *Group work* Compare your answers. Do you think life was better in the old days? Why or why not?

③ SURVEY *City planner*

A What do you think about these things in your city or town? Complete the survey.

	Not enough	OK	Too many/Too much
places to go dancing	☐	☐	☐
places to listen to music	☐	☐	☐
noise	☐	☐	☐
places to sit and have coffee	☐	☐	☐
places to go shopping	☐	☐	☐
parking	☐	☐	☐
public transportation	☐	☐	☐
places to meet new people	☐	☐	☐

B *Group work* Compare your opinions and suggest ways to make your city or town better. Then agree on three improvements.

A: How would you make the city better?
B: There aren't enough places to go dancing. We need more nightclubs.
C: I disagree. There should be fewer clubs. There's too much noise downtown!

④ ROLE PLAY *Could you tell me . . . ?*

Student A: Imagine you are a visitor in your city or town. Write five indirect questions about these categories. Then ask your questions to the hotel receptionist.

Transportation   Restaurants
Sightseeing   Entertainment
Shopping

Student B: You are a hotel receptionist. Answer the guest's questions. Start like this: *Can I help you?*

Change roles and try the role play again.

useful expressions
Let me think. Oh, yes, . . .
I'm not really sure, but I think . . .
Sorry, I don't know.

WHAT'S NEXT?

Look at your Self-assessment again. Do you need to review anything?

3 Time for a change!

1 WORD POWER Houses and apartments

A These words are used to describe houses and apartments. Which are positive (**P**)? Which are negative (**N**)?

cramped

bright ...*P*...	dingy ...*N*...	private ...*P*...
comfortable ...*P*...	expensive ...*N*...	quiet ...*P*...
convenient ...*P*...	huge ...*P*...	safe ...*P*...
cramped ...*N*...	inconvenient ...*N*...	shabby ...*N*...
dangerous ...*N*...	modern ...*P*...	small ...*N*...
dark ...*N*...	noisy ...*N*...	spacious ...*P*...

B *Pair work* Tell your partner two positive and two negative features about your house or apartment.

"My apartment is very dark and a little cramped. However, it's in a safe neighborhood and it's very private."

2 PERSPECTIVES Which would you prefer?

A ▶ Listen to these opinions about houses and apartments.

Apartments are too small for pets.
Apartments aren't big enough for families.
Apartments don't have as many rooms as houses.
Apartments have just as many expenses as houses.
Apartments don't have enough parking spaces.

Houses cost too much money.
Houses aren't as safe as apartments.
Houses aren't as convenient as apartments.
Houses don't have enough closet space.
Houses don't have as much privacy as apartments.

B *Pair work* Look at the opinions again. Which statements do you agree with?

A: I agree that apartments are too small for pets.
B: And they don't have enough parking spaces!

16

3 GRAMMAR FOCUS

Evaluations and comparisons

Evaluations with adjectives
Apartments are**n't** big **enough** for families.
Apartments are **too** small for pets.

Evaluations with nouns
Apartments do**n't** have **enough** parking spaces.
Houses cost **too much** money.

Comparisons with adjectives
Houses are**n't as** convenient **as** apartments.
Houses are **just as** convenient **as** apartments.

Comparisons with nouns
Apartments have **just as many** rooms **as** houses.
Apartments don't have **as much** privacy **as** houses.

A Imagine you are looking for a house or apartment to rent. Read the two ads. Then rewrite the opinions below using the words in parentheses.

Spacious, modern house
3 bedrooms, 1 bathroom; very private; located in quiet suburb; 2-car garage; $950 per month.

Small, older apartment
2 bedrooms, 1 bathroom; located downtown, convenient to the subway; 1 parking space; $500 per month.

1. There are only a few windows. (not enough)
2. It's not bright enough. (too)
3. It has only one bathroom. (not enough)
4. It's not convenient enough. (too)
5. It's not spacious enough. (too)
6. It's too old. (not enough)
7. It isn't safe enough. (too)
8. There's only one parking space. (not enough)

> There aren't enough windows.

B Write comparisons of the house and apartment using these words and *as . . . as*. Then compare with a partner.

noisy	big
bedrooms	expensive
bathrooms	modern
space	convenient
private	parking spaces

> The house isn't as noisy as the apartment.
> The apartment doesn't have as many bedrooms as the house.

C *Group work* Which would you prefer to rent, the house or the apartment? Explain your reasons.

A: I'd rent the apartment because the house costs too much.
B: I'd choose the house. The apartment isn't big enough for my dogs!

4 PRONUNCIATION *Unpronounced vowels*

A ▶ Listen and practice. The vowel immediately after a stressed syllable is frequently not pronounced.

av∅rage   comf∅rtable
diff∅rent   int∅resting
sep∅rate   veg∅table

B Write four sentences using some of the words in part A. Then practice reading them with a partner. Pay attention to unpronounced vowels.

> *In my hometown, the average apartment has two bedrooms.*

5 LISTENING *Capsule hotels*

A ▶ Listen to Brad describe a "capsule hotel." Check (✓) the words that best describe it.

☐ busy   ☐ convenient   ☐ dangerous
☐ comfortable   ☐ cramped   ☐ expensive

B ▶ Listen again. In addition to a bed, what else does the hotel provide? Write four things.

....
....

C *Pair work* Would you like to stay in a capsule hotel? Why or why not?

6 WRITING *A descriptive e-mail*

A Imagine you've just moved to a new apartment. Write an e-mail to a friend comparing your old apartment to your new one.

⬤⬤⬤   Dear Emma

Dear Emma,

How are things with you? My big news is that Mike and I just moved to a new apartment! Do you remember our old apartment? It didn't have enough bedrooms for us. Well, the new apartment has three bedrooms. Also, the old apartment was too cramped, but the new one . . .

B *Pair work* Take turns reading each other's e-mails. Is there anything else you'd like to know about your partner's new apartment?

7 SNAPSHOT

Common Wishes People Have About Their Lives

☐ add more hours to the day

☐ change my appearance

☐ improve my personality

☐ move to a new home

☐ enjoy life more

☑ go back to school

☐ become healthier

☑ find a better job

☑ make new friends

Based on interviews with adults between the ages of 18 and 50

Which of these wishes would be easy to do? Which would be difficult or impossible?
Check (✓) some of the things you would like to do. Then tell a partner why.
What other things would you like to change about your life? Why?

8 CONVERSATION *Making changes*

A ▶ Listen and practice.

Brian: So, are you still living with your parents, Terry?

Terry: I'm afraid so. I wish I had my own apartment.

Brian: Why? Don't you like living at home?

Terry: It's OK, but my parents are always asking me to be home before midnight. I wish they'd stop worrying about me.

Brian: Yeah, parents are like that!

Terry: And they expect me to help around the house. I hate housework. I wish life weren't so difficult.

Brian: So, why don't you move out?

Terry: Hey, I wish I could, but where else can I get free room and board?

B ▶ Listen to the rest of the conversation. What changes would Brian like to make in his life?

9 GRAMMAR FOCUS

Wish ▶

Use **wish** *+ past tense to refer to present wishes.*

I **live** with my parents.
  I wish I **didn't live** with my parents.
  I wish I **had** my own apartment.

I **can't move** out.
  I wish I **could move** out.

Life **is** difficult.
  I wish it **were*** easier.
  I wish it **weren't** so difficult.

My parents **won't stop** worrying about me.
  I wish they **would stop** worrying about me.

After wish, were *is used with all pronouns.*

A Read these facts about people's lives. Then rewrite the sentences using *wish*. (More than one answer is possible.)

1. Diane can't wear contact lenses.   *She wishes she could wear contact lenses.*
2. Beth's class is so boring.   ....
3. My parents can't afford a new car.   ....
4. Dan can't fit into his old jeans.   ....
5. I can't remember my PIN number.   ....
6. Laura doesn't have any free time.   ....

B *Pair work* Think of five things you wish you could change. Then discuss them with your partner.

A: What do you wish you could change?
B: Well, I'm not in very good shape. I wish I were more fit.

10 SPEAKING Wish list

A What do you wish were different about these things? Write down your wishes.

my bedroom	my appearance	my possessions
my school or job	my family	my skills

B *Group work* Compare your wishes. Does anyone have the same wish?

A: I wish my bedroom were a different color. It's not bright enough.
B: Me, too! I wish I could paint my bedroom bright orange.
C: I like the color of my bedroom, but my bed is too small.

11 INTERCHANGE 3 Wishful thinking

Find out more about your classmates' wishes. Go to Interchange 3.

Break Those Bad Habits

Skim the article. What three bad habits does the article mention?

Some people leave work until the last minute, a lot of us can't stop gossiping, and others always arrive to events late. These aren't serious problems, but they are bad habits that can cause trouble. Habits like these waste your time and, in some cases, might even affect your relationships. What can you do about them? Read this advice to end your bad habits for good!

I Can Do It Tomorrow

1 PROBLEM: Do you leave projects until the very last minute and then stay up all night to finish them?

2 SOLUTION: People often put things off because they seem overwhelming. Try dividing the project into smaller steps. After you finish each task, reward yourself with a snack or a call to a friend.

Guess What I Just Heard

3 PROBLEM: Do you try not to talk about other people, but can't help yourself? Do you often feel bad after you've done it?

4 SOLUTION: First, don't listen to gossip. If someone tells you a secret, just say, "Really? I haven't heard that." Then think of some other news to offer – about yourself.

Never On Time

5 PROBLEM: Are you always late? Do your friends invite you to events a half hour early?

6 SOLUTION: Set an alarm clock. For example, if a movie starts at 8:00 and it takes 20 minutes to get to the theater, you have to leave at 7:40. Set the alarm to go off at the time you need to leave.

A Read the article. Then check (✓) the best description of the article.

☐ 1. The article starts with a description and then gives advice.
☐ 2. The article starts with a description and then gives facts.
☐ 3. The article gives the writer's opinion.

B Where do these sentences belong? Write the number of the paragraph where each sentence could go.

.... a. You can also ask a friend to come to your home before the event.
.... b. Ask yourself: "How would I feel if someone told my secrets?"
.... c. Do you ever make up excuses to explain your unfinished work?
.... d. Are you ever so late that the people you're meeting leave?
.... e. You can also ask a friend to call you to ask about your progress.
.... f. Are people afraid to tell you things about themselves?

C *Pair work* Can you think of another way to break each of these bad habits?

4 I've never heard of that!

SNAPSHOT

Favorite Ethnic Dishes

KOREA	BRAZIL	SINGAPORE	LATIN AMERICA
Bulgogi	**Feijoada**	**Fish Head Curry**	**Ceviche**
Beef marinated with soy sauce and other spices	A dish made of black beans, garlic, spices, and pork	A dish made from a fish head cooked in a rich curry sauce	Raw seafood marinated in lime juice and chili peppers

Sources: *Fodor's South America; Fodor's Southeast Asia; www.globalgourmet.com*

Which dishes are made with meat? with fish or seafood?
Have you ever tried any of these dishes? Which ones would you like to try?
What ethnic foods are popular in your country?

2 **CONVERSATION** *Have you ever . . . ?*

A ▶ Listen and practice.

Steve: Hey, this sounds strange – snails with garlic. Have you ever eaten snails?
Kathy: Yes, I have. I had them here just last week.
Steve: Did you like them?
Kathy: Yes, I did. They were delicious! Why don't you try some?
Steve: No, I don't think so.
Waiter: Have you decided on an appetizer yet?
Kathy: Yes. I'll have a small order of the snails, please.
Waiter: And you, sir?
Steve: I think I'll have the fried brains.
Kathy: Fried brains? I've never heard of that! It sounds scary.

B ▶ Listen to the rest of the conversation. How did Steve like the fried brains? What else did he order?

3 · *PRONUNCIATION* Consonant clusters

A ▶ Listen and practice. Notice how the two consonants at the beginning of a word are pronounced together.

/k/	/t/	/m/	/n/	/p/	/r/	/l/
skim	start	smart	snack	spare	brown	blue
scan	step	smile	snow	speak	gray	play

B *Pair work* Find one more word on page 22 for each consonant cluster in part A. Then practice saying the words.

4 · *GRAMMAR FOCUS*

Simple past vs. present perfect ▶

Use the simple past for completed events at a definite time in the past.
Use the present perfect for events within a time period up to the present.

Have you ever **eaten** snails?
  Yes, I **have**. I **tried** them last month.
Did you **like** them?
  Yes, I **did**. They **were** delicious.

Have you ever **been** to a Vietnamese restaurant?
  No, I **haven't**. But I **ate** at a Thai restaurant last night.
Did you **go** alone?
  No, I **went** with some friends.

A Complete these conversations. Then practice with a partner.

1. A: Have you ever .... (be) to a picnic at the beach?
   B: Yes, I .... We .... (cook) hamburgers.

2. A: Have you .... (try) sushi?
   B: No, I .... , but I'd like to.

3. A: Did you .... (have) breakfast today?
   B: Yes, I .... I .... (eat) a huge breakfast.

4. A: Have you ever .... (eat) Mexican food?
   B: Yes, I .... In fact, I .... (eat) some just last week.

5. A: Did you .... (drink) coffee this morning?
   B: Yes, I .... I .... (have) some on my way to work.

B *Pair work* Ask and answer the questions in part A. Give your own information.

5 · *LISTENING* What are they talking about?

▶ Listen to six people ask questions about food and drink in a restaurant. Check (✓) the item that each person is talking about.

1. ☐ water   2. ☐ a meal   3. ☐ soup   4. ☐ coffee   5. ☐ cake   6. ☐ the check
  ☐ bread   ☐ a plate   ☐ pasta   ☐ the meat   ☐ coffee   ☐ the menu

6 SPEAKING *Tell me more!*

Pair work Ask your partner these questions and four
more of your own. Then ask follow-up questions.

Have you ever been on a diet?
Have you ever tried ethnic food?
Have you ever been to a vegetarian restaurant?
Have you ever eaten something you didn't like?

A: Have you ever been on a diet?
B: Yes, I have.
A: Did you lose any weight?
B: No, I didn't. I actually gained weight!

7 INTERCHANGE 4 *Risky business*

Find out some interesting facts about your classmates.
Go to Interchange 4.

8 WORD POWER *Cooking methods*

A How do you cook the foods below? Check (✓) the methods that are
most common in your country. Then compare with a partner.

bake   fry   roast   boil   barbecue   steam

Methods	Foods								
	fish	shrimp	eggs	chicken	beef	potatoes	onions	eggplant	bananas
bake	☐	☐	☐	☐	☐	☐	☐	☐	☐
fry	☐	☐	☐	☐	☐	☐	☐	☐	☐
roast	☐	☐	☐	☐	☐	☐	☐	☐	☐
boil	☐	☐	☐	☐	☐	☐	☐	☐	☐
barbecue	☐	☐	☐	☐	☐	☐	☐	☐	☐
steam	☐	☐	☐	☐	☐	☐	☐	☐	☐

B *Pair work* What's your favorite way to cook or eat the foods in part A?

A: Have you ever steamed fish?
B: No, I haven't. I prefer to bake it.

9 PERSPECTIVES Family cookbook

A ▶ Listen to this recipe for Elvis Presley's favorite peanut butter and banana sandwich.

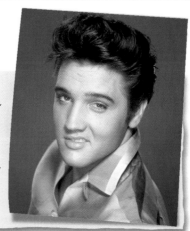

3 tablespoons peanut butter   2 slices of bread
1 banana, mashed   2 tablespoons butter, melted

First, mix the peanut butter and mashed banana together.
Then lightly toast the slices of bread.
Next, spread the peanut butter and banana mixture on the toast.
After that, close the sandwich and put it in a pan with melted butter.
Finally, fry the bread until it's brown on both sides.

B *Pair work* Look at the steps in the recipe again. Number the pictures from 1 to 5. Would you like to try Elvis's specialty?

10 GRAMMAR FOCUS

Sequence adverbs ▶

First, mix the peanut butter and banana together.
Then toast the slices of bread.
Next, spread the mixture on the toast.
After that, put the sandwich in a pan with butter.
Finally, fry the sandwich until it's brown on both sides.

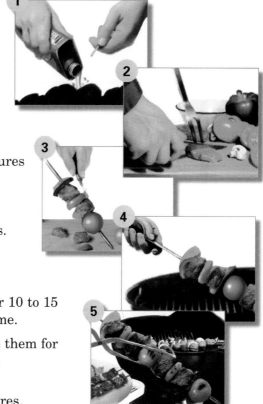

A Here's a recipe for barbecued kebabs. Look at the pictures and number the steps from 1 to 5. Then add a sequence adverb to each step.

☐ .... put the meat and vegetables on the skewers.

☐ .... put charcoal in the barbecue and light it.

☐ .... take the kebabs off the barbecue and enjoy!

☐ .... put the kebabs on the barbecue and cook for 10 to 15 minutes, turning them over from time to time.

☐ .... cut up some meat and vegetables. Marinate them for 20 minutes in your favorite barbecue sauce.

B *Pair work* Cover the recipe and look only at the pictures. Explain each step of the recipe to your partner.

11 LISTENING *Tempting snacks*

A ▶ Listen to people explain how to make these snacks. Which snack are they talking about? Number the photos from 1 to 4.

toasted bagel

guacamole dip

slice of pizza

popcorn

B *Pair work* Choose one of the recipes you just heard about. Can you remember how to make it? Tell your partner.

12 SPEAKING *My favorite snack*

Group work Take turns describing how to make your favorite snack. Then tell the class about the most interesting one.

A: What's your favorite snack?
B: Well, I like to make . . .
C: How do you make it?
B: First, you . . .

13 WRITING *A recipe*

A Read this recipe for a popular Hawaiian dish. Notice how the information is divided into a list of ingredients and how to make the dish.

> ### Lomi Lomi Salmon
>
> ***From the kitchen of** _____*
>
> | | |
> |---|---|
> | 1/4 cup shredded salmon, uncooked | 1 green pepper, diced |
> | 1 white onion, chopped | 3/4 cup vinegar |
> | 2 green onions, sliced | 2 tablespoons sugar |
> | 2 tomatoes, diced | salt and pepper, to taste |
>
> Mix all ingredients together in a bowl. Cover and refrigerate overnight. Eat with rice as a light meal or on crackers as an appetizer.

B Now think of a dish you know how to make. First, write down the ingredients you need. Then describe how to make the dish.

C *Group work* Read and discuss each recipe. Then choose the most interesting recipe to share with the class.

FOOD and MOOD

Skim the article. Then check (✓) the statement you think will be the main idea.
☐ Certain foods cause stress and depression.   ☐ Certain foods affect the way we feel.

We often eat to calm down or cheer up when we're feeling stressed or depressed. Now new research suggests there's a reason: Food changes our brain chemistry. These changes powerfully influence our moods. But can certain foods really make us feel better? Nutrition experts say yes. But what should we eat and what should we avoid? Here are the foods that work the best, as well as those that can make a bad day worse.

To Outsmart Stress

What's good? Recent research suggests that foods that are high in carbohydrates, such as bread, rice, and pasta, can help you calm down. Researchers say that carbohydrates cause the brain to release a chemical called serotonin. Serotonin makes you feel better.

What's bad? Many people drink coffee when they feel stress. The heat is soothing and the caffeine in coffee might help you think more clearly. But if you drink too much, you may become even more anxious and irritable.

To Soothe the Blues

What's good? Introduce more lean meat, chicken, seafood, and whole grains into your diet. These foods have a lot of selenium. Selenium is a mineral that helps people feel more relaxed and happy. You can also try eating a Brazil nut every day. One Brazil nut contains a lot of selenium.

What's bad? When they're feeling low, many people turn to comfort foods – or foods that make them feel happy or secure. These often include things like sweet desserts. A chocolate bar may make you feel better at first, but within an hour you may feel worse than you did before.

A Read the article. The sentences below are false. Correct each sentence to make it true.

1. We often eat when we feel calm.
2. You should drink coffee to relieve stress.
3. Foods like chicken and seafood are high in carbohydrates.
4. Carbohydrates cause the brain to release selenium.
5. Serotonin makes you feel more anxious and irritable.
6. People usually eat comfort foods when they're feeling happy.
7. You shouldn't eat more than one Brazil nut a day.
8. Chocolate will make you feel better.

B *Pair work* What foods do you eat to feel better? After reading the article, which of the advice will you follow?

Units 3-4 Progress check

SELF-ASSESSMENT

How well can you do these things? Check (✓) the boxes.

I can	Very well	OK	A little
Make evaluations and comparisons using nouns and adjectives (Ex. 1)	☐	☐	☐
Listen to, understand, and express wishes (Ex. 2)	☐	☐	☐
Talk about food using the simple past and the present perfect (Ex. 3)	☐	☐	☐
Describe recipes using cooking methods and sequence adverbs (Ex. 4)	☐	☐	☐

1 SPEAKING Apartment ads

A *Pair work* Use the ad and the topics in the box to write an ad for an apartment. Make the apartment sound as good as possible.

Quiet, Private Apartment
Small, but very comfortable, with many windows; located downtown; convenient to stores; 1 bedroom, 1 bathroom, 1-car garage; $300 a month!

age	windows	parking
size	bathroom(s)	cost
location	bedroom(s)	noise

B *Group work* Join another pair. Evaluate and compare the apartments. Which would you prefer to rent? Why?

A: There aren't enough bedrooms in your apartment.
B: But it's convenient.
C: Yes, but our apartment is just as convenient!

2 LISTENING I really need a change!

A ▶ Listen to three people talk about things they wish they could change. Check (✓) the topic each person is talking about.

1. ☐ leisure time   ☐ school   ....
2. ☐ skills   ☐ hobbies   ....
3. ☐ opportunities   ☐ appearance ....

B ▶ Listen again. Write one change each person would like to make.

C *Group work* Use the topics in part A to express some wishes. How can you make the wishes come true? Offer suggestions.

3 SURVEY Food experiences

A Complete the survey with your food opinions and experiences. Then use your information to write questions.

Me	Name
1. I've tried .... , but I didn't really like it. *Have you ever tried* .... *? What did you think of it?*	....
2. One of the best foods I've ever eaten is .... *Is* .... *one of the best foods you've ever eaten?*	....
3. One of the worst foods I've ever eaten is	....
4. I've never tried .... , but I'd like to.	....
5. I've made .... for my friends and family.	....

B *Class activity* Go around the class and ask your questions. Find people who have the same opinions and experiences. Write a classmate's name only once.

A: Have you ever tried peanut butter?
B: Yes, I have.
A: What did you think of it?
B: I didn't really like it.

4 ROLE PLAY Iron Chef

Group work Work in groups of four. Two students are the judges. Two students are the chefs.

Judges: Think of a list of three ingredients for the chefs to use. You will decide which chef creates the best recipe.

Chefs: Think of a recipe using the three ingredients the judges give you and other basic ingredients. Name the recipe and describe how to make it.

"My recipe is called . . . . To make it, first you . . . . Then . . . . Next, ..."

Change roles and try the role play again.

Iron Chef, a TV cooking competition

WHAT'S NEXT?

Look at your Self-assessment again. Do you need to review anything?

5 Going places

What do you like to do on vacation?

Take an exciting trip

☐ visit a foreign country
☒ travel through my own country

Discover something new

☐ take language or cooking lessons
☐ visit museums and art galleries

Stay home

☒ catch up on reading
☐ fix up the house

Enjoy nature

☒ go camping, hiking, or fishing
☒ relax at the beach

Based on information from *U.S. News and World Report*; *American Demographics*

Which activities do you like to do on vacation? Check (✓) the activities.
Which activities did you do on your last vacation?
Make a list of other activities you like to do on vacation. Then compare with a partner.

2 CONVERSATION What are you going to do?

A ▶ Listen and practice.

Julia: I'm so excited! We have two weeks off! What are you going to do?
Nancy: I'm not sure. I guess I'll just stay home. Maybe I'll watch a few DVDs. What about you? Any plans?
Julia: Yeah, I'm going to relax at the beach with my cousin for a couple of weeks. We're going to go surfing every day.
Nancy: Sounds like fun.
Julia: Say, why don't you come with us?
Nancy: Do you mean it? I'd love to! I'll bring my surfboard!

B ▶ Listen to the rest of the conversation. Where are they going to stay? How will they get there?

Future with be going to *and* will

Use be going to + *verb for plans you've decided on.**

What are you **going to do**?
  I'**m going to relax** at the beach.
  We'**re going to go** surfing every day.
  I'**m** not **going to do** anything special.

Use will + *verb for possible plans before you've made a decision.**

What are you **going to do**?
  I'm not sure. I **guess** I'**ll** just **stay** home.
  Maybe I'**ll watch** a few DVDs.
  I don't know. I **think** I'**ll go** camping.
  I **probably won't go** anywhere.

A Complete the conversation with appropriate forms of *be going to* or *will*. Then compare with a partner.

A: Have you made any vacation plans?
B: Well, I've decided on one thing –
   I _going to_ go camping.
A: That's great! For how long?
B: I _going to_ be away for a week.
   I only have five days of vacation.
A: So, when are you leaving?
B: I'm not sure. I _will_ probably leave
   around the end of May.
A: And where _are_ you _going to_ go?
B: I haven't thought about that yet. I guess
   I _will_ go to one of the national parks.
A: That sounds like fun.
B: Yeah. Maybe I _will_ go
   hiking and do some fishing.
A: _Are_ you _going to_ rent a camper?
B: I'm not sure. Actually, I probably _won't_
   rent a camper – it's too expensive.
A: _Are_ you _going to_ go with anyone?
B: No. I need some time alone.
   I _going to_ travel by myself.

B Have you thought about your next vacation? Write answers to these questions. (If you already have plans, use *be going to*. If you don't have fixed plans, use *will*.)

1. How are you going to spend your next vacation?
2. Where are you going to go?
3. When are you going to take your vacation?
4. How long are you going to be on vacation?
5. Is anyone going to travel with you?

I'm going to take my next vacation . . .
OR
I'm not sure. Maybe I'll . . .

C *Group work* Take turns telling the group about your vacation plans.
Use your information from part B.

WORD POWER Travel planning

A Complete the chart. Then add one more word to each category.

backpack	first-aid kit	overnight bag	shorts	vaccination
cash	hiking boots	passport	suitcase	visa
credit card	medication	plane ticket	traveler's checks	windbreaker

Clothing	Money	Health	Documents	Luggage
Hiking boots	cash	First-aid kit	passport	Backpack
shorts	credit card	medication	Plane ticket	overnight bag
windbreaker	travelers checks	vaccination	visa	suitcase
personal check	sun		I.D.	duffel bag

B *Pair work* What are the five most important items you need for these vacations:
a trip to a foreign country? a rafting trip? a mountain-climbing expedition?

5 INTERCHANGE 5 Fun vacations

Decide between two vacations. Go to the back of the book. Student A find
Interchange 5A; Student B find Interchange 5B.

6 PERSPECTIVES Travel advice

A ▶ Listen to these pieces of advice from experienced travelers.

> *"You should tell the driver where you're going before you get on. And you have to have exact change for the fare."* — Patrick

> *"In most countries, you don't have to have an international driver's license, but you must have a license from your own country. You also need to be over 21."* — Jackie

> *"You should try some of the local specialties, but you'd better avoid the stalls on the street."* — Paul

> *"You ought to pack a first-aid kit and any medication you need. You shouldn't drink water from the tap."* — Susan

> *"You ought to keep a copy of your credit card numbers at the hotel. And you shouldn't carry a lot of cash when you go out."* — Luis

B *Pair work* Look at the advice again. What topic is each person talking about?

A: Paul is probably talking about food, because he mentions "specialties."
B: And I think Jackie is giving advice about . . .

7 GRAMMAR FOCUS

Modals for necessity and suggestion ▷

Describing necessity
You **must** have a driver's license.
You **need to** make a reservation.
You **have to** get a passport.
You **don't have to** get a visa.

Giving suggestions
You**'d better** avoid the stalls on the street.
You **ought to** pack a first-aid kit.
You **should** try some local specialties.
You **shouldn't** carry a lot of cash.

A Choose the best advice for someone who is going on vacation. Then compare with a partner.

1. You 'd better make hotel reservations in advance. It might be difficult to find a room after you get there. (have to / 'd better)
2. You must to carry identification with you. It's the law! (must / should)
3. You should buy a round-trip plane ticket because it's cheaper. (must / should)
4. You shouldn't pack too many clothes. You won't have room to bring back any gifts. (don't have to / shouldn't)
5. You need to check out of most hotel rooms by noon if you don't want to pay for another night. (need to / ought to)
6. You ought to buy a new suitcase because your old one is getting shabby. (have to / ought to)

B *Pair work* Imagine you're going to travel abroad. Take turns giving each other advice.

"You must get the necessary vaccinations."

1. You . . . get the necessary vaccinations.
2. You . . . take your ATM card with you.
3. You . . . get the visa required for each country.
4. You . . . forget to pack your camera.
5. You . . . have a passport to enter a foreign country.
6. You . . . change money before you go. You can do it when you arrive.

C *Group work* What advice would you give someone who is going to study English abroad? Report your best ideas to the class.

8 PRONUNCIATION Linked sounds with /w/ and /y/

 Listen and practice. Notice how some words are linked by a /w/ sound, and other words are linked by a /y/ sound.

/w/
You should know about local conditions.

/y/
You shouldn't carry a lot of cash.

/w/
You ought to do it right away.

/y/
You must be over 18 years old.

9 LISTENING Tourist tips

A ▶ Listen to an interview with a spokeswoman from the New York City Visitor's Center. Check (✓) the four topics she discusses.

☐ planning a trip   ☐ safety   ☐ money   ☐ eating out   ☐ tours   ☐ history

B ▶ Listen again. For each topic, write one piece of advice she gives.

10 WRITING Travel suggestions

A Imagine someone is going to visit your town, city, or country. Write a letter giving some suggestions for sightseeing activities.

> Dear Rosa,
>
> I'm so glad you're going to visit Prague! As you know, Prague is the capital of the Czech Republic. It's a very beautiful city, so you should bring your camera. Also, you ought to bring some good shoes, because we're going to walk a lot. It will be warm, so you don't have to pack . . .

B *Pair work* Exchange letters. Is there anything else the visitor needs to know about (food, money, business hours, etc.)?

11 DISCUSSION Dream vacation

A *Pair work* You just won a free 30-day trip around the world. Discuss the following questions.

When will you leave and return?
Which route will you take?
Where will you choose to stop? Why?
How many days will you spend in each place?

B *Pair work* What do you need to do before you go? Discuss these issues.

visas   hotel reservations   vaccinations
money   what to buy and pack

A: We'd better find out if we need to get any visas.
B: Yes, and I think we ought to buy some guidebooks.

Getting Away From It All

Check (✓) the statements you think are true. Then scan the article to check your answers.

- ☐ *Wear layers of clothing to go backpacking.*
- ☐ *Put heavy items at the top of your backpack.*

Mike O'Brien has been backpacking for over 20 years. He often spends up to 30 days at a time outdoors. In a recent interview with *Outdoor Magazine*, he offered some expert tips for new backpackers.

OM: Why do you spend so much

MO: Backpacking and camping are my favorite things to do. It can get difficult at times, but I just love getting away from it all.

OM: what do all beginners need to k

MO: The two most important things to know are how to dress comfortably and how to pack your equipment well.

OM: How should people dress

MO: They need to understand the purpose of outdoor clothing. Clothes need to keep you warm in the cold, block the wind, and keep you dry in the rain. In hot environments, clothes should also protect you from the sun. You don't have control over the weather or the temperature. So you should dress in light layers of clothing. That way, if you are hot, you can take off clothes. And if you are cold, you can add clothes.

OM: And how should they pack

MO: Access and balance are the keys to packing well. First, access: Don't bury things you need – such as extra clothes, food, or water – at the bottom of your backpack. Second, balance: Remember, you're going to wear your backpack. It has to be balanced or you could fall over! Don't make your pack too heavy at the top or bottom. It's best to keep the heaviest items close to your back.

OM: Any final words?

MO: Yes. Have fun! That's the only reason to do it!

A Read the article. Then write these questions in the appropriate place.

1. What do all beginners need to know?
2. And how should they pack for a trip?
3. Any final words?
4. How should people dress for backpacking?
5. Why do you spend so much time in the wilderness?

B Complete the summary with information from the article.

Mike O'Brien is an expert backpacking. For beginners, he says that there are two important things to remember: dress comfort and pack well. Because you don't have control over weather, you should dress in light layers. The keys to packing are Access and balance. Don't bury thing u need at the bottom of your backpack. And don't make your pack heavy.

C ***Group work*** Choose a sport or activity you know well. What "expert" tips would you offer beginners?

6 OK. No problem!

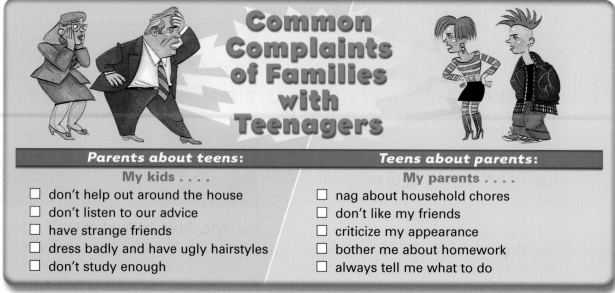

Common Complaints of Families with Teenagers

Parents about teens:	Teens about parents:
My kids	**My parents . . . .**
☐ don't help out around the house	☐ nag about household chores
☐ don't listen to our advice	☐ don't like my friends
☐ have strange friends	☐ criticize my appearance
☐ dress badly and have ugly hairstyles	☐ bother me about homework
☐ don't study enough	☐ always tell me what to do

Based on information from *America Online's Parent Resource Site*

Which complaints seem reasonable? Which ones seem unreasonable? Why?
Check (✓) a complaint you have about a family member.
What other complaints do people sometimes have about family members?

2 CONVERSATION *Turn down the TV!*

A ▶ Listen and practice.

Mr. Field: Jason . . . Jason! Turn down the TV, please.
Jason: Oh, but this is my favorite program!
Mr. Field: I know. But it's very loud.
Jason: OK. I'll turn it down.
Mr. Field: That's better. Thanks.
Mrs. Field: Lisa, please pick up your things.
They're all over the floor.
Lisa: In a minute, Mom. I'm on the phone.
Mrs. Field: All right. But do it as soon as you hang up.
Lisa: OK. No problem!
Mrs. Field: Goodness! Were we like this when
we were kids?
Mr. Field: Definitely!

B ▶ Listen to the rest of the conversation.
What complaints do Jason and Lisa have
about their parents?

36

③ GRAMMAR FOCUS

Two-part verbs; will for responding to requests ▶

With nouns	With pronouns	Requests and responses
Turn down the TV.	**Turn** it **down**.	Please turn down the music.
Turn the TV **down**.		OK. I'**ll** turn it down.
Pick up your things.	**Pick** them **up**.	Pick up your clothes, please.
Pick your things **up**.		All right. I'**ll** pick them up.

A Complete the requests with these words. Then compare with a partner.

the books

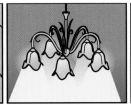
the toys

the radio

your jacket

the TV

your boots

the yard

the lights

the trash

the dog

1. Pick up ....*the toys*........ , please.
2. Turn ...*the lights*... off, please.
3. Clean ...*the yard*... up, please.
4. Please put *the books* away.
5. Please turn down ...*the radio*... .

6. Please take off ...*your boots*...
7. Hang *your jacket* up, please.
8. Please take out ...*the trash*...
9. Please let ...*the dog*... out.
10. Turn on *the tv* , please.

B *Pair work* Take turns making the requests above. Respond with pronouns.

A: Pick up the toys, please.
B: No problem. I'll pick them up.

④ PRONUNCIATION *Stress in two-part verbs*

A ▶ Listen and practice. Both words in a two-part verb receive equal stress.

○	○	○	○		○	○	○	○		○	○	○
Pick	up	the	toys.		Pick	the	toys	up.		Pick	them	up.
Turn	off	the	light.		Turn	the	light	off.		Turn	it	off.

B Write four more requests using the verbs in Exercise 3.
Then practice with a partner. Pay attention to stress.

5 WORD POWER Household chores

A Find a phrase that is usually paired with each two-part verb.
(Some phrases go with more than one verb.) Then add one more
phrase for each verb.

the garbage the mess the newspapers your coat
the groceries the microwave the towels your laptop

clean up	_the mess_		take out	_the garbage_	
hang up	_your coat_	_the towels_	throw out	_the garbage_	
pick up	_the mess_	_newspapers_	turn off	_your laptop_	_the microwave_
put away	_the groceries_	_the garbage_	turn on	_your laptop_	_the microwave_

B What requests can you make in each of these rooms? Write four
requests and four unusual excuses. Use two-part verbs.

the kitchen the living room
the bathroom the bedroom

C *Pair work* Take turns making
the requests you wrote in part B.
Respond by giving an unusual excuse.

A: Kim, please clean up your mess
in the kitchen.
B: Sorry, I can't clean it up right now.
I have to take the cat out for a walk.

6 LISTENING Family life

A ▶ Listen to the results of a survey about family life.
For each question, write men (**M**), women (**W**), boys (**B**),
or girls (**G**).

Who is the messiest in the house? ....
Who does most of the work in the kitchen? ....
Who usually takes out the garbage? ....
Who worries most about expenses? ....

B ▶ Listen again. According to the survey, what specific
chores do men, women, boys, and girls usually do?
Take notes.

C *Group work* Discuss the questions in parts A and B.
Who does these things in your family?

7 PERSPECTIVES *Would you mind . . . ?*

A ▶ Listen to the requests people make of their neighbors. Have you ever made a similar request? Has anyone ever asked you to do these things?

"Could you please tell me the next time you have a party? I'd like to make sure I'm not at home."

"Can you turn the stereo off, please? The walls are really thin, so the sound goes through to my apartment."

"Would you mind closing the door behind you and making sure it locks? We don't want any strangers to enter the building."

"Would you please tell your guests to use the visitor parking spaces? A lot of cars have been using my space recently."

"Would you mind not putting your garbage in front of your door? It's not very pleasant to see it in the hallway."

B Look at the requests again. Which are reasonable? Which are unreasonable?

8 GRAMMAR FOCUS

Requests with modals and Would you mind . . . ? ▶

Modal + simple form of verb	Would you mind . . . + gerund
Can you **turn** the stereo **off**?	**Would** you **mind turning** the stereo **down**?
Could you **close** the door, please?	**Would** you **mind closing** the door, please?
Would you please **take** your garbage **out**?	**Would** you **mind not putting** your garbage here?

A Match the requests with the appropriate responses. Then compare with a partner and practice them. (More than one answer may be possible.)

1. Could you lend me twenty dollars? ..d..
2. Can you get me a sandwich? ..e–f..
3. Can you help me move to my new house? ..e–f..
4. Would you mind not sitting here? ..C..
5. Could you move your car from my space? ..b..
6. Would you mind not talking so loudly? ..a..

a. We're sorry. We'll talk more quietly.
b. I'm sorry. I'll do it right away.
c. Sorry. I didn't realize this seat was taken.
d. Are you kidding? I don't have any cash.
e. I'm really sorry, but I'm busy.
f. Sure, no problem. I'd be glad to.

B *Pair work* Take turns making the requests in part A. Give your own responses.

C *Class activity* Think of five unusual requests. Go around the class and make your requests. How many people accept? How many refuse?

A: Could you lend me your toothbrush?
B: Oh, I'm sorry. I don't have it with me.

9 *SPEAKING* Apologies

A Think of three complaints you have about your neighbors. Write three requests you want to make. Choose from these topics or use ideas of your own.

garbage   guests   noise   parking   pets   security

B *Pair work* Take turns making your requests. The "neighbor" should apologize by giving an excuse, admitting a mistake, or making an offer or promise.

A: Would you mind not putting your garbage in the hallway?
B: Oh, I'm sorry. I didn't realize it bothered you.

different ways to apologize	
give an excuse	"I'm sorry. I didn't realize . . ."
admit a mistake	"I forgot I left it there."
make an offer	"I'll take it out right now."
make a promise	"I promise I'll . . . / I'll make sure to . . ."

10 *INTERCHANGE 6* That's no excuse!

How good are you at apologizing? Go to Interchange 6.

11 *WRITING* A set of guidelines

A *Pair work* Imagine that you live in a large apartment building. Use complaints from Exercise 9 and your own ideas to write a set of eight guidelines.

> ### The Riverview Apartments
>
> *Please read the following tenant association guidelines. Feel free to contact Joseph (#205) or Tina (#634) if you have any questions.*
>
> 1. *The pool summer hours are 8 A.M. to 9 P.M. Please clear the area by 9 P.M.*
>
> 2. *Can everyone make an effort to keep the laundry room clean? Please pick up after yourself!*
>
> 3. *Would you mind not picking the flowers in the garden? They're for everyone's enjoyment.*

B *Group work* Take turns reading your guidelines aloud. What is the best new guideline? the worst one?

Neighbor vs. Neighbor

Read the situations in the list below. What would you do in each situation?

- The woman in the apartment upstairs plays her piano after midnight.

- The family across the street never cleans up their yard. The garbage blows into your yard.

- The guy next door always parks his car in front of your driveway.

Have things like this ever happened to you? If so, you may ask yourself, "Who are these people? Why are they doing these things to me?"

These days, many people don't know their neighbors. Sometimes we share a friendly wave or say hello, but a lot of people don't even know their neighbors' names! When you don't know someone, it's easy to build up frustration and resentment. You think, "Maybe they like to annoy me," or "Maybe they do it deliberately."

Believe it or not, your neighbors probably don't mean to irritate you. Often, they don't even know that they're getting on your nerves. So before you take extreme measures to fix the problem, you should discuss it with them first.

When you approach your neighbors, you should talk to them in a friendly manner. Compliment their children or do something else to make them feel good. Then explain the situation. And if you can think of a simple solution, suggest it.

If talking doesn't work, ask another person to help. This person can listen to both sides of the story and help you and your neighbor resolve the situation.

Finally, sometimes it's a good idea to avoid the problem. Depending on the issue, it might be best to just stay out of your neighbor's way.

A Read the article. Find the words in *italics* in the article. Then match each word with its meaning.

- _b_ 1. *resentment*
- _d_ 2. *deliberately*
- _f_ 3. *irritate*
- _e_ 4. *measure*
- _a_ 5. *manner*
- _c_ 6. *resolve*

- a. a way of behaving
- b. anger that grows over time
- c. end a problem or difficulty
- d. on purpose
- e. a step taken in order to achieve something
- f. bother or annoy

B Check (✓) the questions that the article answers. Then find sentences in the article that support your answers.

- ☐ 1. Why don't many people know their neighbors?
- ☐ 2. Why do we become angry at neighbors?
- ☐ 3. What are some extreme measures you can take to solve a problem?
- ☑ 4. How should you approach a neighbor about a problem?
- ☑ 5. What can you do when discussion doesn't work?

C *Pair work* Have you ever had a problem with a neighbor, classmate, or co-worker? How did you resolve it?

Units 5–6 Progress check

SELF-ASSESSMENT

How well can you do these things? Check (✓) the boxes.

I can	Very well	OK	A little
Listen to and understand plans using *be going to* and *will* (Ex. 1)	☐	☐	☐
Ask and answer questions about plans using *be going to* and *will* (Ex. 2)	☐	☐	☐
Give travel advice using modals for necessity and suggestion (Ex. 2)	☐	☐	☐
Make requests using two-part verbs (Ex. 3)	☐	☐	☐
Apologize, give excuses, and accept or refuse requests using *will* (Ex. 3, 4)	☐	☐	☐
Make requests using modals and *Would you mind . . . ?* (Ex. 4)	☐	☐	☐

1 LISTENING Summer plans

A ▶ Listen to Judy, Paul, and Brenda describe their summer plans.
What is each person going to do?

	Summer plans	Reason
1. Judy	....	....
2. Paul	....	....
3. Brenda	....	....

B ▶ Listen again. What is the reason for each person's choice?

2 DISCUSSION Planning a vacation

A *Group work* Imagine you are going to go on vacation.
Take turns asking and answering these questions.

A: **Where are you going to go on your next vacation?**
B: I'm going to go to Hawaii.
C: **What are you going to do?**
B: I'm going to go camping and hiking. Maybe I'll try rock climbing.
A: **Why did you choose that?**
B: Well, I really enjoy nature. And I want to do something different!

B *Group work* What should each person do to prepare
for his or her vacation? Give each other advice.

3 ROLE PLAY *Excuses, excuses!*

Student A: Your partner was supposed to do some things, but didn't. Look at the pictures, and make a request about each one.

Student B: You were supposed to do some things, but didn't. Listen to your partner's requests. Apologize and either accept the request or give an excuse.

A: You left the towels on the floor. Please hang them up.
B: I'm sorry. I forgot about them. I'll hang them up right now.

Change roles and try the role play again.

4 GAME *Could you do me a favor?*

A Write three requests on separate cards. Put an *X* on the back of two of the cards.

> Can you cook dinner tonight?

> Could you get me a cup of coffee?

> Would you mind closing the window?

B *Class activity* Shuffle all the cards together. Take three new cards.

Go around the class and take turns making requests with the cards. Hold up each card so your classmate can see the back.

When answering:
X on the back = refuse the request and give an excuse
No *X* = accept the request

> Can you cook dinner tonight?

> I'm sorry, I can't. I'm . . .

WHAT'S NEXT?

Look at your Self-assessment again. Do you need to review anything?

7 What's this for?

SNAPSHOT

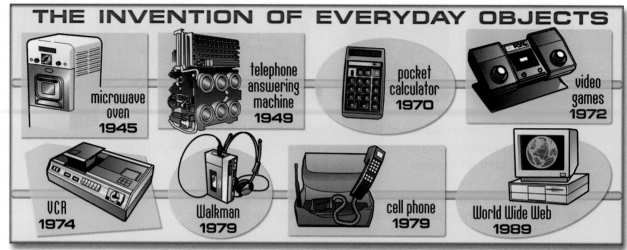

THE INVENTION OF EVERYDAY OBJECTS

microwave oven **1945**

telephone answering machine **1949**

pocket calculator **1970**

video games **1972**

VCR **1974**

Walkman **1979**

cell phone **1979**

World Wide Web **1989**

Sources: *The People's Almanac Presents the 20th Century*; *www.about.com*

Circle the things that you use every day or almost every day.
Which invention do you think is the most important? the least important?
What are some other things you use every day?

2 **PERSPECTIVES** *Computer usage*

A How do you use your computer, or how would you use a computer if you had one? Listen and respond to the statements.

Rate Your Computer Usage

I use/would use a computer	Often	Sometimes	Hardly ever	Never
to send and receive e-mails	☐	☐	☐	☐
for paying bills	☐	☐	☐	☐
to play games	☐	☐	☐	☐
to find information on the Web	☐	☐	☐	☐
for doing school assignments	☐	☐	☐	☐
to learn languages	☐	☐	☐	☐
for writing letters	☐	☐	☐	☐
to check the weather	☐	☐	☐	☐
to read the news	☐	☐	☐	☐
for downloading music	☐	☐	☐	☐

B *Pair work* Compare your answers. Are your answers similar or different?

3 GRAMMAR FOCUS

Infinitives and gerunds for uses and purposes ▶

Infinitives	Gerunds
I use my computer **to send** e-mails.	I use my computer **for sending** e-mails.
Computers are often used **to pay** bills.	Computers are often used **for paying** bills.

A What do you know about this technology? Complete the phrases in column A with information from column B. Then compare with a partner. (More than one answer is possible.)

A

1. Satellites are used . . .
2. Robots are sometimes used . . .
3. You can use a cell phone . . .
4. People use the Internet . . .
5. DNA fingerprinting is used . . .
6. CD-ROMs are used . . .

B

study the world's weather
perform dangerous tasks
read the latest weather report
transmit telephone calls
send text messages
identify criminals
make travel reservations
transmit television programs
store an encyclopedia

> Satellites are used to study the world's weather.
> Satellites are used for studying the world's weather.

B *Group work* Think of three more items of technology. Then talk about possible uses for each one.

"You can use DVD players to watch movies and to play CDs."

4 PRONUNCIATION Syllable stress

A ▶ Listen and practice. Notice which syllable has the main stress.

● ○ ○	○ ● ○	○ ○ ●
satellite	invention	CD-ROM
Internet	assignment	engineer
photograph	computer	entertain
. . . .	. . . .	. . . .
. . . .	. . . .	. . . .

B ▶ Where is the stress in these words? Add them to the columns in part A. Then listen and check.

languages   understand   telephone   transmission   robotics   VCR

5 **WORD POWER** *The world of computers*

A Complete the chart with words and phrases from the list. Add one
more to each category. Then compare with a partner.

✓ browse Web sites	drag and drop	keyboard	scan photographs
cut and paste	geek	monitor	surf the net
disk drive	hacker	mouse	technophile
double-click (on)	highlight text	play games	whiz

People who are "into" computers	Types of computer hardware	Fun things to do with a computer	Things to do with a mouse
		browse Web sites	

B *Group work* Discuss how computers have changed
our lives. Ask and answer questions like these:

How do computers make your life easier?
    more difficult?
How do computers affect the way you spend
    your free time?
How do computers influence the kinds of jobs
    people have?
What kinds of problems do computers cause?
Do you know anyone who is a computer whiz?
Are hackers a problem where you live?

 6 **LISTENING** *Off-line – and proud!*

A ▶ Guess the answers to the questions below.
Then listen to a radio program about the Internet and
check your answers.

What percentage of the population never uses the
Internet? What kinds of people don't use the Internet?

B ▶ Listen to the rest of the program. Then answer
these questions.

What does the term "net evaders" mean?
What are "Internet dropouts"?
Why do some people become Internet dropouts?

7 CONVERSATION Can I borrow your phone?

A  Listen and practice.

Jenny: Can I borrow your phone to call my boss?
Richard: I can't believe you still don't have a cell
      phone. Here you go.
Jenny: Thanks. Now, what do I need to do?
Richard: First of all, be sure to turn it on. And don't
      forget to dial the area code.
Jenny: OK, I can see the number, but I can't
      hear anything.
Richard: That's because you haven't pressed the
      "call" button.
Jenny: Oh, good. It's ringing.
Richard: Try not to get too excited. You'll probably
      get his voice mail.
Jenny: You're right. It's a recording.
Richard: Make sure to hit the "end" button or else
      you'll leave our conversation on his voice mail!

B Listen to the rest of the conversation. Who does
Jenny want to call next?

8 GRAMMAR FOCUS

> ### Imperatives and infinitives for giving suggestions
>
> **Be sure to** turn it on.   **Remember to** pay the bill every month.
> **Don't forget to** dial the area code.   **Try not to** talk for too long.
> **Make sure to** hit the "end" button.

A Look at these suggestions. Which ones refer to an alarm system (**AS**)?
a cell phone (**CP**)? a laptop computer (**LC**)? (More than one answer is
sometimes possible.) Then think of another suggestion for each thing.

1. Try to keep it closed to protect the screen. ....
2. Don't forget to write down your secret code. ....
3. Remember to turn it off as soon as you come in the door. ....
4. Try not to get it wet or the keys may get stuck. ....
5. Make sure to set it each time you leave home. ....
6. Remember to recharge the batteries before they die. ....
7. Be sure to turn it off before bed or a call may wake you up. ....

B *Group work* Take turns giving suggestions for using the items in
part A. Use these phrases.

Make sure to . . .	Try to . . .	Remember to . . .
Be sure not to . . .	Try not to . . .	Don't forget to . . .

What's this for? • **47**

9 SPEAKING Free advice

A ▶ Listen to people give advice about three of the things below. Write the name of each item in the chart.

CD Walkman

in-line skates

motorbike

ATM card

camcorder

personal watercraft

Item	Advice
1.	....
2.	....
3.	....

B ▶ Listen again. Complete the chart. Then compare with a partner.

C *Pair work* What do you know about the other things in part A? What advice can you give about them?

10 INTERCHANGE 7 Talk radio

Give callers to a radio program some advice. Go to Interchange 7.

11 WRITING A note giving instructions

A Imagine a friend is going to stay in your home while you're on vacation. Think of three unusual things you want him or her to do. Then write a note giving instructions.

Su Jin,
    Thanks again for agreeing to house-sit for me. Please remember to do these three things: First, make sure to feed Owen, my pet snake, or else he'll escape and move around the house. Also, don't forget to . . .

B *Group work* Take turns reading your **notes** aloud. Who gave the most unusual instructions?

A Day in Your Life – In the Year 2020

Scan the article. Then add the correct heading to each paragraph.
Communicating   Shopping   Relaxing   Eating   Getting Around   Working

People used to know more or less how their children would live. Now things are changing so quickly that we don't even know what our own lives will be like in a few years. What follows is how experts see the future.

....

You're daydreaming behind the wheel of your car, but that's OK. You have it on automatic pilot, and with its high-tech computers, your car knows how to get you home safely.

....

You head for the kitchen when you get home. You ordered groceries by computer an hour ago, and they've been delivered. You paid for them before they arrived. The money was automatically deducted from your bank account. Nobody uses cash anymore.

....

What's for lunch? In the old days, you used to stop off to get a hamburger or pizza. Now you use your diagnostic machine to find out which foods your body needs. Your food-preparation machine makes you a salad.

....

After lunch, you go down the hall to your home office. Here you have everything you need to do your work. You never have to commute to work anymore.

....

Your information screen says that you've received a message from a co-worker in Brazil. You set your computer to translate Portuguese into English. Your co-worker's face appears on the screen, and the translation appears at the bottom.

....

You finish working and go back to your living room. You turn on the television and look through the list of new movies. It's like having a video store in your home. How about a classic tonight? Maybe *Back to the Future*?

A Read the article. Check (✓) True or False for each statement about the future. Then write true information for each false statement.

True False

☐	✔	1. You need to pay attention while driving.	*Your car has automatic pilot.*
☐	☐	2. You pay for your groceries when they arrive.	....
☐	☐	3. People don't use cash anymore.	....
☐	☐	4. You usually buy a hamburger or pizza for lunch.	....
☐	☐	5. You need to go to the office every day.	....
☐	☐	6. You and your co-workers have to speak the same language.	....
☐	☐	7. When you get a message, you can see the sender's face.	....
☐	☐	8. You have to go to a video store to rent movies.	....

B *Pair work* Which changes sound the most interesting? the most useful? Are there any changes that you don't like?

8 Let's celebrate!

1 ## SNAPSHOT

Holidays and Festivals

Chinese New Year
January or February
Chinese people celebrate
with firecrackers and
lion dances.

Valentine's Day
February 14
People in many countries give
chocolates, flowers, or jewelry to
the people they love.

Children's Day
May 5
Japanese families put up colored
streamers shaped like fish, in
honor of their children.

Day of the Dead
November 2
Mexican families offer food
to the dead and then have
a meal in a cemetery.

Source: *Reader's Digest Book of Facts*

Which of these holidays celebrate people? Which celebrate events?
Do you celebrate these or similar holidays in your country?
What other special days do you have? What's your favorite holiday or festival?

2 ## WORD POWER

Pair work Complete the word map. Add one more word to each category.
Then describe a recent celebration using some of the words.

anniversary
cake
cards
dancing
fireworks
flowers
fruit punch
parade
party
presents
roast turkey
wedding

Special occasions

Activities

Celebrations

Special food and drink

Things we give/receive

A: I went to a friend's birthday party recently. There was live music and dancing.
B: What kind of music did they play?

3 PERSPECTIVES *Special days*

A ▶ Listen to people discuss some special days of the year.

"My favorite holiday is Thanksgiving. It's a day when North Americans celebrate the harvest. Everyone in the family gets together at our house. I cook a large turkey and serve it with cranberry sauce."

"February 14 is the day when people give cards and presents to the ones they love. I'm really looking forward to Valentine's Day this year! I already have the perfect gift for my boyfriend."

"I can't wait until the end of the year! New Year's Eve is a night when I have fun with my friends. We usually have a party at someone's house. We stay up all night and then go out for breakfast in the morning."

B *Pair work* Look at the statements again. Do you like any of the holidays? Which ones?

4 GRAMMAR FOCUS

> ### Relative clauses of time ▶
>
> | | |
> |---|---|
> | Thanksgiving is **a day** | **when** North Americans celebrate the harvest. |
> | February 14 is **the day** | **when** people give cards to the ones they love. |
> | New Year's Eve is **a night** | **when** I have fun with my friends. |

A How much do you know about these days and months? Complete the sentences in column A with information from column B. Then compare with a partner.

A

1. New Year's Day is a day when ....
2. April Fools' Day is a day when ....
3. May and June are the months when ....
4. Valentine's Day is a day when ....
5. Labor Day is a day when ....
6. February is the month when ....

B

a. Brazilians celebrate Carnaval.
b. people have parties with family and friends.
c. many young adults choose to get married.
d. people in many countries honor workers.
e. people express their love to someone.
f. people sometimes play tricks on friends.

B Complete these sentences with your own information. Then compare with a partner.

Winter is the season . . .
Birthdays are days . . .
Spring is the time of year . . .

Mother's Day is a day . . .
July and August are the months . . .
A wedding anniversary is a time . . .

5 LISTENING Carnaval time

Carnaval in Brazil

A ▶ Mike has just returned from Brazil. Listen to him talk about Carnaval. What did he enjoy most about it?

B ▶ Listen again and answer these questions.

What is Carnaval?
How long does it last?
When is it?
What is the samba?

6 SPEAKING Special days

A *Pair work* Choose your three favorite holidays. Tell your partner why you like each one.

A: I really like New Year's Day.
B: What do you like about it?
A: Well, it's a day when I make my New Year's resolutions.

B *Class activity* Take a class vote. What are the most popular holidays in your class?

Day of the Dead in Mexico

Chinese New Year

7 WRITING A travel guide

A Write a paragraph for a travel magazine about a festival or celebration where you live. When is it? How do people celebrate it? What should a visitor be sure to see and do?

> The annual fireworks festival in Yenshui, Taiwan, occurs on the last day of the New Year celebration. This is the first full moon of the new lunar year. It's a day when people explode fireworks in the streets, paint their faces, and dress up as ...

B *Pair work* Read your partner's paragraph. What do you like about it? Can you suggest anything to improve it?

8 CONVERSATION Wedding day

A ▶ Listen and practice.

Jill: Your wedding pictures are really beautiful, Emiko.

Emiko: Thank you. Those pictures were taken right after the ceremony.

Jill: Where was the ceremony?

Emiko: At a shrine. When people get married in Japan, they sometimes have the ceremony at a shrine.

Jill: That's interesting. Were there a lot of people there?

Emiko: Well, usually only family members and close friends go to the ceremony. But afterward we had a reception with family and friends.

Jill: So, what are receptions like in Japan?

Emiko: There's a big dinner, and after the food is served, the guests give speeches or sing songs.

Jill: It sounds like fun.

Emiko: It really is. And then, before the guests leave, the bride and groom give them presents.

Jill: The guests get presents?

Emiko: Yes, and the guests give money to the bride and groom.

B ▶ Listen to the rest of the conversation. What did the bride and groom give each guest?

9 PRONUNCIATION Stress and rhythm

A ▶ Listen and practice. Notice how stressed words and syllables occur with a regular rhythm.

○   ○   ○   ○   ○   ○

When people get married in Japan, they sometimes have the ceremony at a shrine.

B ▶ Listen to the stress and rhythm in these sentences. Then practice them.

After the ceremony, there's a reception with family and friends.

Before the guests leave, the bride and groom give them presents.

The guests usually give money to the bride and groom.

10 GRAMMAR FOCUS

Adverbial clauses of time ▶

When people get married in Japan,	they sometimes have the ceremony at a shrine.
After the food is served,	the guests give speeches or sing songs.
Before the guests leave,	the bride and groom give them presents.

A What do you know about wedding customs in North America?
Match these phrases with the information below.

1. Before a man and woman get married, they usually ....
2. When a couple gets engaged, the man often ....
3. Right after a couple gets engaged, they usually ....
4. When a woman gets married, her family usually ....
5. When people are invited to a wedding, they almost always ....
6. Right after a couple gets married, they usually ....

a. pays for the wedding and reception.
b. go on a short trip called a "honeymoon."
c. give the bride and groom a gift or some money.
d. gives the woman a diamond ring.
e. begin to plan the wedding.
f. "date" each other for about a year.

B *Pair work* What happens when people get married in your country?
Complete the statements in part A with your own information.
Pay attention to stress and rhythm.

11 INTERCHANGE 8 *Once in a blue moon*

How do your classmates celebrate special events?
Go to Interchange 8.

12 SPEAKING *That's an interesting custom.*

A *Group work* Do you know any interesting customs related to the
topics below? Explain a custom and discuss it with your classmates.

births   marriages   courtship   seasons   good luck

A: I know a custom from the Philippines. When a
boy courts a girl, he stands outside her house
and sings to her.
B: What kinds of songs does he sing?
C: Romantic songs, of course!

B *Class activity* Tell the class the most interesting
custom you talked about in your group.

Unique CUSTOMS

Look at the photos. What do you think is happening in each picture?

1 January 17 is **St. Anthony's Day** in Mexico. It's a day when people ask for protection for their animals by bringing them to church. But before the animals go into the church, the people usually dress them up in flowers and ribbons.

2 On August 15 of the lunar calendar, Koreans celebrate **Chusok**, also known as Korean Thanksgiving. It's a day when people give thanks for the harvest. Korean families honor their ancestors by going to their graves to take them rice and fruit and clean the gravesites.

3 Long ago in India, a princess who needed help sent her silk bracelet to an emperor. Although he did not arrive in time to help her, he kept the bracelet as a sign of the bond between them. Today in India, during the festival of **Rakhi**, men promise to be loyal to their women. In exchange, the women give them a bracelet of silk, cotton, or gold thread.

4 One of the biggest celebrations in Argentina is **New Year's Eve**. On the evening of December 31, families get together and have a big meal. At midnight, fireworks explode everywhere and continue throughout the night. This is a day when friends and families meet for parties, which last until the next morning.

5 On the evening of February 3, people in Japan celebrate the end of winter and the beginning of spring. This is known as **Setsubun**. Family members throw dried beans around their homes, shouting, "Good luck in! Evil spirits out!" After they throw the beans, they pick them up and eat one bean for each year of their age.

A Read the article. Then answer these questions.

1. How do people in Mexico dress their animals on St. Anthony's Day?
2. Why do Koreans celebrate Chusok?
3. Why do Indian women give men a bracelet for the festival of Rakhi?
4. What do families in Argentina do on New Year's Eve?
5. What do Japanese families do during Setsubun?

B What do these words refer to? Write the correct word(s).

1. them (par. 1, line 2) .... 4. them (par. 3, line 5) ....
2. It (par. 2, line 2) .... 5. This (par. 4, line 4) ....
3. their (par. 2, line 4) .... 6. them (par. 5, line 5) ....

C *Pair work* Do you know of a celebration or custom that is similar to those in the article? Describe it.

Units 7–8 Progress check

SELF-ASSESSMENT

How well can you do these things? Check (✓) the boxes.

I can	Very well	OK	A little
Describe uses and purposes using infinitives and gerunds (Ex. 1)	☐	☐	☐
Give instructions and advice using imperatives and infinitives (Ex. 2)	☐	☐	☐
Describe special days using relative clauses of time (Ex. 3)	☐	☐	☐
Listen to and understand information using adverbial clauses of time (Ex. 4)	☐	☐	☐
Ask and answer questions using adverbial clauses of time (Ex. 5)	☐	☐	☐

1 GAME What is it?

A *Pair work* Think of five familiar objects. Write a short description of each object's use and purpose. Don't write the name of the objects.

> It's electronic. You connect it to your TV. It's used for playing movies. You can also use it to record TV shows.

B *Group work* Take turns reading your descriptions and guessing the objects. Keep score. The pair with the most correct answers wins.

2 ROLE PLAY Stressful situations

Student A: Choose one situation below. Decide on the details and answer Student B's questions. Then get some advice. Start like this: *I'm really nervous. I'm . . .*

going on a job interview
What's the job?
What are the responsibilities?
Who is interviewing you?

going on a first date
Who is it with?
Where are you going?
When are you going?

giving a speech
What is it about?
Where is it?
How many people will be there?

Student B: Student A is telling you about a situation. Ask the appropriate questions above. Then offer two pieces of advice.

Change roles and try the role play again.

useful expressions	
Try to . . .	Try not to . . .
Remember to . . .	Be sure to . . .
Don't forget to . . .	Make sure to . . .

③ SPEAKING My own holiday

A *Pair work* Choose one of these imaginary holidays or create your own.
Then write a description of the holiday. Answer the questions below.

World Smile Day

All-You-Can-Eat Cake Day

Be Late For Something Day

What is the name of the holiday? When is it? How do you celebrate it?

> *World Smile Day is a day when you have to smile at everyone. It's on June 15,*
> *the last day of school. People have parties, and sometimes there's a parade!*

B *Group work* Read your description to the group. Then vote on the best holiday.

④ LISTENING Marriage customs

A ▶ Listen to some information about unusual marriage customs.
Check (✓) True or False for each statement.

	True	False
1. When two women of a tribe in Paraguay want to marry the same man, they have a boxing match.	☐	☐
2. When people get married in Malaysia, they have to eat cooked rice.	☐	☐
3. In Italy, before a couple gets married, a friend or relative releases two white doves.	☐	☐
4. In some parts of India, when people get married, water is poured over them.	☐	☐

B ▶ Listen again. Correct the statements that you marked false.

⑤ DISCUSSION In your country . . .

Group work Talk about marriage in your country. Ask these questions and others of your own.

How old are people when they get married?
What happens after a couple gets engaged?
What happens during the ceremony?
What do the bride and groom wear?
What kind of food is served at the reception?
What kinds of gifts do people usually give?

a Korean wedding

WHAT'S NEXT?

Look at your Self-assessment again. Do you need to review anything?

9 Back to the future

PAST, PRESENT, AND *FUTURE*	*Past*	*Present*	*Future*
Transportation	railroads and ocean liners	cars and jet airplanes	flying cars and commercial space flights?
Communications	the telephone and the postal system	cell phones and e-mail	video phones and audio letters?
Entertainment	radio and movies	television and computer games	3-D television and virtual reality games?

Sources: *New York Public Library Book of Chronologies; New York Public Library Desk Reference*

Which of these past and present developments are the most important? Why?
Do you think any of the future developments could happen in your lifetime?
How will clothing and music be different in the future? Suggest two differences.

2 CONVERSATION *This neighborhood has changed!*

A ▶ Listen and practice.

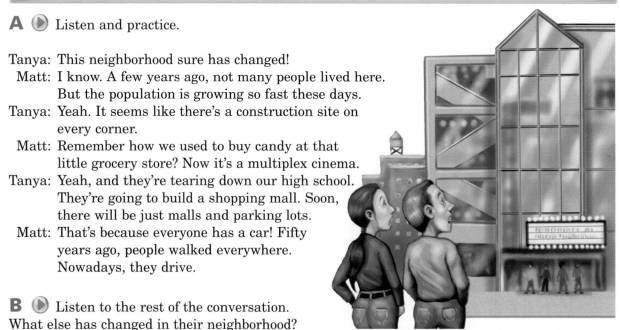

Tanya: This neighborhood sure has changed!
  Matt: I know. A few years ago, not many people lived here. But the population is growing so fast these days.
Tanya: Yeah. It seems like there's a construction site on every corner.
  Matt: Remember how we used to buy candy at that little grocery store? Now it's a multiplex cinema.
Tanya: Yeah, and they're tearing down our high school. They're going to build a shopping mall. Soon, there will be just malls and parking lots.
  Matt: That's because everyone has a car! Fifty years ago, people walked everywhere. Nowadays, they drive.

B ▶ Listen to the rest of the conversation.
What else has changed in their neighborhood?

3 GRAMMAR FOCUS

Time contrasts

Past	Present	Future
A few years ago, not many people **lived** here.	These days, the population **is growing** so fast.	Soon, there **will be** a lot of shopping malls.
People **used to shop** at grocery stores.	Today, people **shop** at supermarkets.	In twenty years, people **might buy** groceries by computer.
Fifty years ago, people **walked** everywhere.	Nowadays, people **drive** their cars instead.	In the future, people **are going to use** cars even more.

A Match the phrases in column A with the appropriate information from column B. Then compare with a partner.

A

1. Before the automobile, ...
2. Before there were supermarkets, ...
3. About five hundred years ago, ...
4. In most offices today, ...
5. In many cities nowadays, ...
6. Soon, ...
7. In the next hundred years, ...
8. Sometime in the future, ...

B

a. people used to shop at small stores.
b. pollution is becoming a serious problem.
c. most people are going to work at home.
d. people didn't travel as much from city to city.
e. there will probably be cities in space.
f. people work more than 40 hours a week.
g. people played the first game of golf.
h. doctors might find a cure for the common cold.

B Complete the phrases in part A with your own information. Then compare with a partner.

4 PRONUNCIATION *Intonation in statements with time phrases*

A ▶ Listen and practice. Notice the intonation in these statements beginning with a time phrase.

In the past, very few people used computers.

Today, people use computers all the time.

In the future, there will be a computer in every home.

B *Pair work* Complete these statements with your own information. Then read your statements to a partner. Pay attention to intonation.

As a child, I used to . . .   Next year, I'm going to . . .
Five years ago, I . . .   In five years, I'll . . .
Nowadays, I . . .   In ten years, I might . . .

5 LISTENING For better or for worse

A Listen to people discuss changes. Check (✓) the topic each person talks about.

Topic		Change	Better or worse?	
1. ☐ population	☐ environment	....	☐	☐
2. ☐ transportation	☐ cities	....	☐	☐
3. ☐ families	☐ shopping	....	☐	☐

B Listen again. Write down the change and if things are better or worse now.

6 SPEAKING Changing times

Group work How have things changed? How will things be different in the future? Choose two of these topics. Then discuss the questions below.

education   fashion   housing   shopping   technology
entertainment   food   medicine   sports   transportation

What was it like in the past?
What is it like today?
What will it be like in the future?

A: In the past, a lot of people made their own clothes.
B: Nowadays, they often order things online.
C: In the future, . . .

7 WRITING A description of a person

A *Pair work* Interview your partner about his or her past, present, and hopes for the future.

B Write a paragraph describing how your partner has changed. Make some predictions about the future. Don't write your partner's name.

> She used to be the quietest girl in the class. Now, she's in the drama club and loves to watch soap operas. One day, she'll be a successful actress. She'll be famous, and will star in movies and on TV. I think she'll . . .

C *Class activity* Read your paragraph to the class. Can they guess who it is about?

8 PERSPECTIVES *Who wants to make money?*

A Listen to some possible consequences of getting a high-paying job. Check (✓) the statements you agree with.

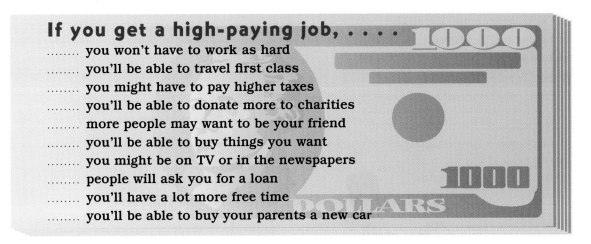

If you get a high-paying job, ...
.... you won't have to work as hard
.... you'll be able to travel first class
.... you might have to pay higher taxes
.... you'll be able to donate more to charities
.... more people may want to be your friend
.... you'll be able to buy things you want
.... you might be on TV or in the newspapers
.... people will ask you for a loan
.... you'll have a lot more free time
.... you'll be able to buy your parents a new car

B *Pair work* Look at the statements again. Which are advantages of getting a high-paying job? Which are disadvantages?

"I think the first one is an advantage. I don't like to work very hard."

9 GRAMMAR FOCUS

Conditional sentences with if clauses ▷

Possible situation + simple present	*Consequence + future with* will, may, *or* might
If you get a high-paying job,	you **won't have to work** as hard.
If you don't have to work as hard,	you'**ll have** a lot more free time.
If you have a lot more free time,	you **might get** bored.
If you get bored,	you **may have to look for** another job.

A Match the clauses in column A with the appropriate information from column B. Then compare with a partner.

A

1. If you eat less sugar, ...
2. If you walk to work every day, ...
3. If you don't get enough sleep, ...
4. If you own a pet, ...
5. If you don't get married, ...

B

a. you may feel more relaxed.
b. you might feel healthier.
c. you'll stay in shape without joining a gym.
d. you'll have more money to spend on yourself.
e. you won't be able to stay awake in class.

B Add your own information to the clauses in column A. Then practice with a partner.

"If you eat less sugar, you'll lose weight."

10 WORD POWER Consequences

A *Pair work* Can you find two consequences for each possible event?
Complete the chart with information from the list.

be able to buy expensive clothes
feel better about yourself
feel hungry a lot
feel jealous sometimes
feel safer in your home
have to give up your favorite snack
get requests for loans from friends
have to learn a new language
have to take it out for walks
lose touch with old friends

Possible event	Consequences
buy a large dog	....
fall in love	....
go on a diet	....
inherit a lot of money	....
move to a foreign country	....

B *Group work* Share your answers with the group. Can you think of
one more consequence for each event?

11 SPEAKING Unexpected consequences

A *Group work* Choose three possible events from Exercise 10.
One student completes an event with a consequence. The next
student adds a consequence. Suggest at least five consequences.

A: If you buy a large dog, you'll have to take it out for walks every day.
B: If you take it out for walks every day, you might have an accident.
C: If you have an accident, you may have to go to the hospital.
D: If you go to the hospital, you won't be able to take care of your dog.
A: If you aren't able to take care of your dog, you'll probably have to give it away.

B *Class activity* Who has the most interesting consequences for each event?

12 INTERCHANGE 9 Consider the consequences

Give your opinion about some issues. Go to Interchange 9 at the back of the book.

Are you in love?

What is the difference between "having a crush" on someone and falling in love?

You think you're falling in love. You're really attracted to a certain person. But this has happened before, and it was just a "crush." How can you tell if it's real this time? Here's what our readers said:

If you're falling in love, . . .

♥ you'll find yourself talking to or telephoning the person for no reason. (You might pretend there's a reason, but often there's not.)

♥ you'll find yourself bringing this person into every conversation. ("When I was in Mexico – ," a friend begins. You interrupt with, "My boyfriend made a great Mexican dinner last week.")

♥ you might suddenly be interested in things you used to avoid. ("When a woman asks me to tell her all about football, I know she's fallen in love," said a TV sports announcer.)

OK, so you've fallen in love. But falling in love is one thing, and staying in love is another. How can you tell, as time passes, that you're still in love? If you stay in love, your relationship will change. You might not talk as much about the person you are in love with. You might not call him or her so often. But this person will nevertheless become more and more important in your life.

You'll find that you can be yourself with this person. When you first fell in love, you were probably afraid to admit certain things about yourself. But now you can be totally honest. You can trust him or her to accept you just as you are. Falling in love is great – staying in love is even better!

A Read the article. Where do you think it is from? Check (✓) the correct answer.

☐ a newspaper ☐ a magazine ☐ an advice column ☐ an advertisement

B What things happen when you're falling in love compared to staying in love? Complete the chart.

Falling in love	Staying in love
1.	1. ....
2.	2. ....
3.	3. ....

C *Pair work* Which is more difficult – falling in love or staying in love? Can you think of other signs of being in love?

10 I don't like working on weekends!

1 SNAPSHOT

EIGHT IMPORTANT JOB SKILLS

Here are some skills that employers look for.

1. Can you **solve problems?**	5. Are you good at **math and science?**
2. Do you **work well with people?**	6. Can you **manage money well?**
3. Can you **use a computer?**	7. Do you **speak other languages?**
4. Can you **teach others** how to do things?	8. Can you **manage other people?**

Source: U.S. Department of Labor

Which of these skills do you think are most important? Why?
Check (✓) the skills that you think you have.
Look at the skills you checked. What jobs do you think you might be good at?

2 CONVERSATION *I need a job!*

A ▶ Listen and practice.

Dan: I'm so broke. I really need to find a job!
Brad: So do I. Do you see anything good listed on the Internet?
Dan: How about this? A door-to-door salesperson to sell baby products.
Brad: Like diapers and things? No, thanks. And anyway, I'm not good at selling.
Dan: Well, I am! I might check that one out. Oh, here's one for you. An assistant entertainment director on a cruise ship.
Brad: That sounds like fun. I like traveling, and I've never been on a cruise ship.
Dan: It says here you have to work every day while the ship is at sea.
Brad: That's OK. I don't mind working long hours if the pay is good. What's the phone number?
Dan: It's 555-3455.

B ▶ Listen to Brad call about the job.
What else does the job require?

64

3 GRAMMAR FOCUS

Gerunds; short responses

Affirmative statements with gerunds	Agree	Disagree	Other verbs or phrases followed by gerunds
I like **traveling**.	So do I.	Oh, I don't.	love
I hate **working** on weekends.	So do I.	Really? I like it.	enjoy
I'm good at **using** a computer.	So am I.	Gee, I'm not.	be interested in
Negative statements with gerunds			
I don't **mind working** long hours.	Neither do I.	Well, I do.	
I'm not **good at selling**.	Neither am I.	I am!	
I can't **stand making** mistakes.	Neither can I.	Oh, I don't mind.	

A *Pair work* Match the phrases in columns A and B to make statements about yourself. Then take turns reading your sentences and giving short responses.

A

1. I don't like ....
2. I'm not very good at ....
3. I'm good at ....
4. I hate ....
5. I can't stand ....
6. I'm interested in ....
7. I don't mind ....
8. I enjoy ....

B

a. talking on a cell phone.
b. working with a group or team.
c. solving other people's problems.
d. sitting in long meetings.
e. commuting by bicycle.
f. eating lunch out every day.
g. managing my time.
h. learning foreign languages.

A: I don't like commuting by bicycle.
B: Neither do I.

B *Group work* Complete the phrases in column A with your own information. Then take turns reading your statements. Ask questions to get more information.

4 PRONUNCIATION Unreleased and released /t/ and /d/

A Listen and practice. Notice when the sound /t/ or /d/ at the end of a word is followed by a consonant, it is unreleased. When it is followed by a vowel sound, it is released.

Unreleased

She's not good at math and science.

I hate working on Sundays.

You need to manage money well.

Released

He's not a good artist.

They really hate it!

I need a cup of coffee.

B *Pair work* Write three sentences starting with *I'm not very good at* and *I don't mind*. Then practice the sentences. Pay attention to the unreleased and released sounds /t/ and /d/.

5 LISTENING Job hunting

A ▶ Listen to people talk about the kind of work they are looking for. Check (✓) the job that would be best for each person.

1. Bill
   - ☐ flight attendant
   - ☐ teacher
   - ☐ songwriter

2. Shannon
   - ☐ lawyer
   - ☐ bookkeeper
   - ☐ doctor

3. Ben
   - ☐ marine biologist
   - ☐ model
   - ☐ architect

B ▶ Listen again. Answer these questions.

1. What is Bill's attitude toward making money?
2. What does most of Shannon's family do for a living?
3. What has Ben done to break into movies?

6 SPEAKING Chores

A *Pair work* Interview your partner about these chores. Check (✓) his or her answers.

How do you feel about . . . ?	I enjoy it.	I don't mind it.	I hate it.
doing your homework	☐	☐	☐
washing the dishes	☐	☐	☐
cleaning your room	☐	☐	☐
making phone calls	☐	☐	☐
washing your clothes	☐	☐	☐
organizing your desk	☐	☐	☐
typing your school reports	☐	☐	☐
buying groceries	☐	☐	☐
ironing your clothes	☐	☐	☐
commuting to and from school	☐	☐	☐

B *Pair work* Imagine the government is offering a robot to all students. Each robot can do four chores for two students. Decide which chores you want your robot to do.

A: I want the robot to do my homework for me.
   I can't stand doing my homework.
B: Neither can I. But I hate cleaning my room even more!

C *Group work* There is a shortage of robots. Each robot can only do two chores for four students. Discuss the things you want your robot to do.

7 INTERCHANGE 10 Dream job

Decide which job to apply for. Go to Interchange 10 at the back of the book.

8 WORD POWER Personality traits

A Which of these adjectives are positive (**P**)? Which are negative (**N**)?

bad-tempered	...N...	hardworking	....
creative	....	impatient	....
critical	....	level-headed	....
disorganized	....	moody	....
efficient	....	punctual	....
forgetful	....	reliable	....
generous	....	strict	....

bad-tempered

disorganized

B *Pair work* Tell your partner about people you know with these personality traits.

"My neighbor is bad-tempered. Sometimes she . . . "

C ▶ Listen to four conversations. Then check (✓) the adjective that best describes each person.

1. a boss
   - ☐ creative
   - ☐ forgetful
   - ☐ serious

2. a co-worker
   - ☐ unfriendly
   - ☐ generous
   - ☐ strange

3. a teacher
   - ☐ moody
   - ☐ patient
   - ☐ hardworking

4. a relative
   - ☐ bad-tempered
   - ☐ disorganized
   - ☐ reliable

9 PERSPECTIVES Job profiles

A ▶ Listen to these people answer the question, "What kind of work would you like to do?" What job does each person talk about?

"Well, I think I'd make a good journalist because I'm good at writing. When I was in college, I worked as a reporter for the school newspaper. I really enjoyed writing different kinds of articles."

"I know what I *don't* want to do! A lot of my friends work in the stock market, but I could never be a stockbroker because I can't make decisions quickly. I don't mind working hard, but I'm terrible under pressure!"

"I'm still in school. My parents want me to be a teacher, but I'm not sure yet. I guess I could be a teacher because I'm very creative. I'm also very impatient, so maybe I shouldn't work with kids."

B *Pair work* Look at the interviews again. Which job would you choose?

10 GRAMMAR FOCUS

Clauses with because ▶

The word because *introduces a cause or reason.*

I'd make a good journalist **because I'm good at writing.**
I could be a teacher **because I'm very creative.**
I wouldn't want to be a teacher **because I'm very impatient.**
I could never be a stockbroker **because I can't make decisions quickly.**

A Complete the sentences in column A with appropriate information from column B. Then compare with a partner.

A

1. I wouldn't want to be a nurse ....
2. I'd like to be a novelist ....
3. I could never be an accountant ....
4. I would make a bad waiter ....
5. I could be a flight attendant ....

B

a. because I don't like hospitals.
b. because I really enjoy traveling.
c. because I have a terrible memory.
d. because I'm terrible with numbers.
e. because I love creative writing.

B *Group work* Think about your personal qualities and skills. Then complete these statements. Take turns discussing them with your group.

I could never be a . . . because . . .
I wouldn't mind working as a . . . because . . .
I'd make a good . . . because . . .

C *Class activity* Choose some statements made by members of your group. Share them with the rest of the class.

"I have a terrible memory."

11 WRITING *A cover letter for a job application*

A Imagine you can apply for one of the jobs in this unit. Write a short cover letter for a job application.

Attention: Mr. Yoshioka, Personnel Director, Executive Air Lines

Dear Mr. Yoshioka,
I am responding to your recent advertisement in *The Post* for a bilingual international flight attendant. I think I'd make a good flight attendant for Executive Air Lines because I'm a very friendly person and I really love traveling. I also enjoy meeting people. As you can see from my résumé, I've had a lot of experience working with tourists. I worked at . . .

B *Pair work* Exchange papers. If you received this letter, would you invite the applicant for a job interview? Why or why not?

Find the Job That's Right for You!

Look at the photo and skim the list below. What personality type do you think best describes the person in the picture?

1 Nearly 50% of all workers in the United States have jobs they aren't happy with. Don't let this happen to you! If you want to find the right job, don't rush to look through the classified ads in the newspaper. Instead, sit down and think about yourself. What kind of person are you? What makes you happy?

2 According to psychologist John Holland, there are six types of personalities. Nobody is just one personality type, but most people are mainly one type. For each type, there are certain jobs that might be right and others that are probably wrong.

3 Considering your personality type can help you make the right job decision. Liz is a good example. Liz knew she wanted to do something for children. She thought she could help children as a school counselor or a lawyer. She took counseling and law courses – and hated them. After talking to a career counselor, she realized the problem was that she's an Artistic type. Liz studied film, and she now produces children's TV shows – and loves it.

The **Realistic** type is practical and likes working with machines and tools.

The **Investigative** type is curious and likes to learn, analyze situations, and solve problems.

The **Artistic** type is imaginative and likes to express himself or herself by creating art.

The **Social** type is friendly and likes helping or training other people.

The **Enterprising** type is outgoing and likes to persuade or lead other people.

The **Conventional** type is careful and likes to follow routines and keep track of details.

A Read the article. Then find these sentences in the article. Decide whether each sentence is the main idea or a supporting idea in that paragraph. Check (✓) the correct boxes.

	Main idea	Supporting idea
1. Nearly 50% of all workers . . . they aren't happy with. (par. 1)	☐	☐
2. According to psychologist . . . types of personalities. (par. 2)	☐	☐
3. For each type, there are . . . that are probably wrong. (par. 2)	☐	☐
4. Considering your personality . . . the right job decision. (par. 3)	☐	☐
5. After talking to a career counselor, . . . an Artistic type. (par. 3)	☐	☐

B For each personality type, write two examples of appropriate jobs. Then explain your answers to a partner.

Realistic	Investigative	Artistic	Social	Enterprising	Conventional
. . . .	. . . .	. . . .	. . . .	. . . .	. . . .
. . . .	. . . .	. . . .	. . . .	. . . .	. . . .

C *Group work* What personality type do you think you are? Does your group agree?

Units 9–10 Progress check

SELF-ASSESSMENT

How well can you do these things? Check (✓) the boxes.

I can	Very well	OK	A little
Ask and answer questions about changes using time contrasts (Ex. 1)	☐	☐	☐
Describe possibilities using conditional sentences with *if* clauses (Ex. 2)	☐	☐	☐
Listen to and understand descriptions of abilities and personality traits (Ex. 3)	☐	☐	☐
Ask and answer questions about job preferences and skills using gerunds (Ex. 4)	☐	☐	☐
Give reasons using clauses with *because* (Ex. 4)	☐	☐	☐

1 SPEAKING Past, present, and future

A *Pair work* Think of one more question for each category. Then interview a partner.

Appearance   What did you use to look like? Can you describe yourself now?
              What do you think you'll look like in the future?

Free time   Did you have a hobby as a child? What do you like to do these days?
              How are you going to spend your free time next year?

B *Group work* Share one interesting thing about your partner.

2 GAME Truth and consequences

A Add one event and one consequence to the lists below.

Event	Consequence
☐ you move to a foreign country	☐ buy you a gift
☐ it's sunny tomorrow	☐ feel jealous sometimes
☐ it's cold tomorrow	☐ have to learn a new language
☐ you give me $10	☐ go to the beach
☐ you don't call me later	☐ get really angry
☐ you go on a diet	☐ feel hungry a lot
☐ you fall in love	☐ stay home
☐	☐ ....

B *Class activity* Go around the class and make sentences. Check (✓) each *if* clause after you use it. The student who uses the most clauses correctly wins.

3 LISTENING *Good or bad?*

A ▶ Listen to Louisa and Tim discuss four jobs. Write down the jobs and check (✓) if they would be good or bad at them.

Job	Good	Bad	Reason
1. Louisa	☐	☐	....
....	☐	☐	....
2. Tim	☐	☐	....
....	☐	☐	....

B ▶ Listen again. What reasons do they give?

4 DISCUSSION *Job profile*

A Prepare a personal job profile. Write your name, skills, and job preferences. Think about the questions below. Then compare with a partner.

Are you good at . . . ?
communicating with people
solving problems
making decisions quickly
speaking foreign languages

Do you . . . ?
have any special skills
have any experience
have a good memory
manage money well

Do you like . . . ?
traveling
working with a team
wearing a uniform
working long hours

A: Are you good at communicating with people?
B: Sure. I enjoy talking to people.
A: So do I. I like meeting new people and . . .

B *Group work* Make suggestions for possible jobs based on your classmates' job profiles. What do you think of their suggestions for you?

A: Hmm. Juan could be an executive because he likes solving problems and making decisions quickly.
B: No way! I could never be an executive. I'm too disorganized!

WHAT'S NEXT?

Look at your Self-assessment again. Do you need to review anything?

11 It's really worth seeing!

1 SNAPSHOT

The Great Wall of China was begun in 214 B.C. It is the largest structure ever built.

The Colosseum in Rome was opened in 80 A.D. It was sometimes filled with water for ship battles.

Machu Picchu in Peru was constructed around 1400 A.D. It was probably a home for the Inca royal family.

The Statue of Liberty in New York was opened in 1886. It was a gift to the United States from the people of France.

The Eiffel Tower in Paris was completed in 1889. It was built for the 100th anniversary of the French Revolution.

Source: *World Book Encyclopedia*

Which landmark did people live in? Which was a gift? Which was used for events?
What else do you know about these places?
What are the three most famous landmarks in your country?

2 PERSPECTIVES The Empire State Building

A How much do you know about the Empire State Building?
Check (✓) the statements you think are true.

☐ 1. The Empire State Building was designed by an American architect.
☐ 2. It was officially opened by the president of the United States in 1931.
☐ 3. It is located in New York City.
☐ 4. The construction of the building took five years.
☐ 5. It cost $2 million to build.
☐ 6. There are 102 floors in the building.
☐ 7. It is the tallest building in the world.
☐ 8. It was featured in the movie *King Kong*.

B Now listen and check your answers. What information is the most surprising?

GRAMMAR FOCUS

Passive with by (simple past) ▶

The passive changes the focus of a sentence.
For the simple past, use the past of be + past participle.

Active
The president **opened** the building in 1931.
An American architect **designed** the building.

Passive
It **was opened by** the president in 1931.
It **was designed by** an American architect.

A Do you know who created these popular works? Match the phrases in column A with the appropriate information from column B. Then compare with a partner.

A

1. *The Kiss* ....
2. The song "Yesterday" ....
3. The film *Schindler's List* ....
4. The novel *Pride and Prejudice* ....
5. The opera *Carmen* ....

B

a. was composed by Georges Bizet.
b. was painted by Gustav Klimt.
c. was written by Jane Austen.
d. was directed by Steven Spielberg.
e. was recorded by the Beatles.

B *Pair work* Change these sentences into passive sentences with *by*.
Then take turns reading them aloud.

1. Frédéric Bartholdi designed the Statue of Liberty in 1884.
2. Marie Curie discovered radium in 1898.
3. Gabriel García Márquez wrote *One Hundred Years of Solitude* in 1971.
4. Woo Paik produced the first digital HDTV (high-definition television) in 1991.
5. Salma Hayek played Frida Kahlo in the movie *Frida* in 2002.

INTERCHANGE 11 *Who is this by?*

Who created these well-known works? Go to Interchange 11.

5 PRONUNCIATION *The letter o*

A Listen and practice. Notice how the letter *o* is pronounced in the following words.

/o/	/ou/	/u:/	/ʌ/
not	no	do	one
top	don't	food	love
....	....	....	....
....	....	....	....

B ▶ How is the letter *o* pronounced in these words? Write them in the correct column in part A. Then listen and check your answers.

come   done   lock   own   shot   soon   who   wrote

6 LISTENING *Ancient monuments*

▶ Listen to three tour guides describe some very old monuments. Take notes to answer the questions below. Then compare with a partner.

1 the Pyramids

2 Machu Picchu

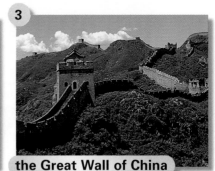

3 the Great Wall of China

Who built them?
Why were they built?

How big is the city?
When was it discovered?

Why was it built?
How long is it?

7 WORD POWER *Where is it from?*

A Complete the chart. Then add one more word to each category.

cars   microchips
cattle   oysters
chickens   rice
✓ coffee   sheep
corn   shrimp
✓ lobsters   televisions

Farmed	Grown	Manufactured	Raised
lobsters	*coffee*		

B *Group work* Talk about things that are found in your country.

"We grow coffee. We also manufacture cars."

8 CONVERSATION *I need some information.*

A ▶ Listen and practice.

Kelly: Hello?
John: Oh, hello. I need some information. What currency is used in the European Union?
Kelly: Where?
John: The European Union.
Kelly: I think the euro is used in most of the EU.
John: Oh, right. And is English spoken much there?
Kelly: I really have no idea.
John: Huh? Well, what about credit cards? Are they accepted everywhere?
Kelly: How would I know?
John: Well, you're a travel agent, aren't you?
Kelly: What? This is a hair salon. You have the wrong number!

B *Pair work* Use information about a country you know to act out the conversation.

9 GRAMMAR FOCUS

Passive without by *(simple present)* ▶

For the simple present, use the present of be + past participle.

Active	Passive
They **use** the euro in most of the European Union.	The euro **is used** in most of the EU.
They **speak** English in many European countries.	English **is spoken** in many European countries.
They **manufacture** a lot of cars in Europe.	A lot of cars **are manufactured** in Europe.

A Complete this passage using the simple present passive form.

Many crops .... (grow) in Taiwan. Some crops .... (consume) locally, but others .... (export). Tea .... (grow) in cooler parts of the island and rice .... (cultivate) in warmer parts. Fishing is also an important industry. A wide variety of seafood .... (catch). Many people .... (employ) in the electronics and textile industries.

B Complete the sentences. Use the passive of these verbs.

grow   make up   manufacture   raise   speak   use

1. French and English .... in Canada.
2. A lot of rice .... in Vietnam.
3. The U.S. .... of 50 states.
4. A lot of sheep .... in New Zealand.
5. Cars and computers .... in Korea.
6. The U.S. dollar .... in Ecuador.

C *Pair work* Use the passive of the verbs in part B to talk about your country and other countries you know.

10 LISTENING Colombia

A ▶ Listen to a short talk about Colombia. Complete the chart.

Facts about Colombia	
Location	....
Population	....
Language	....
Industries	....
Agricultural products	....

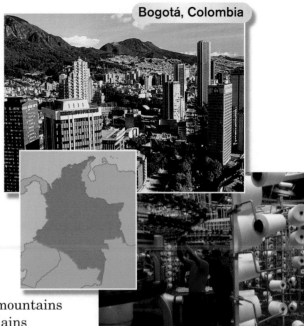
Bogotá, Colombia

B ▶ Listen again. Check (✓) the things the speaker mentions about Colombia.

☐ beaches   ☐ volcanoes   ☐ snow-capped mountains
☐ rivers   ☐ lakes   ☐ hot lowland plains

11 SPEAKING True or false?

A *Pair work* Choose a country. Then answer these questions. Include one false statement.

Where is it located?   What currency is used?
What cities are found there?   What famous tourist attraction is found there?
What languages are spoken?   What products are exported?

B *Class activity* Give a short talk like the one in Exercise 10 about the country you chose. Can the class identify the false statement?

12 WRITING A guidebook introduction

A Make an information chart like the one in Exercise 10 about a country you know. Then write an introduction for a guidebook about the country.

> Vietnam is located in Southeast Asia. It has a population of over 80 million people. Vietnamese is the official language. The country has many beautiful beaches, high mountains, and busy cities. Rice is grown in . . .

B *Group work* Exchange papers. Is any important information missing? Do you want to visit the country?

A Guide To Unusual Museums

Look at the pictures and scan the article. Where do you think you can see very old objects? a working factory? historic cooking tools?

1 Do you like museums? Have you been to the Louvre in Paris, the Museum of Anthropology in Mexico City, or any of those other "must see" museums? Well, now it's time to go off the beaten path.

The Kimchi Museum
Seoul, Korea

2 If you don't know about kimchi, a trip to the Kimchi Museum is an eye-opening experience. The museum was founded in 1986 to highlight Korea's rich kimchi culture. The exhibit includes displays of cooking utensils and materials related to making, storing, and eating the famous pickled vegetables. The museum also provides details about the history and nutritional benefits of Korea's most beloved side dish. Finally, stop by the souvenir shop to try various types of kimchi.

The Museum of Gold
Bogotá, Colombia

3 If you want to see beautiful objects, the Museum of Gold is *the* place. It holds one of South America's most stunning collections. Because the exhibits sparkle so brightly, you can actually take photographs without using a flash on your camera! Not everything is made of gold, though. Among the exhibits are ancient pre-Columbian items. Many of them are made from a mixture of gold and copper, known as *tumbaga*.

The Chocolate Museum
Cologne, Germany

4 The Chocolate Museum will teach you everything about chocolate – from cocoa bean to candy bars. You'll learn about chocolate's 3,000-year history and discover how it was once used as money in South America. A real chocolate factory shows you how chocolate is made. After you've finished the tour, you can sample a complimentary drink of rich, gooey pure chocolate – perfect for those with a sweet tooth.

A Read the article. Find the words in *italics* in the article. Then circle the meaning of each word or phrase.

1. When you *go off the beaten path*, you **do something unusual** / **go somewhere far away**.
2. When something is *founded*, it is **started** / **discovered**.
3. When something is *stunning*, it is extremely **attractive** / **large**.
4. When something is *ancient*, it is **very old** / **common**.
5. When something is *complimentary*, it is **free of charge** / **very expensive**.
6. When something is *gooey*, it is **light and refreshing** / **thick and sticky**.

B Where do these sentences belong? Write the number of the paragraph where each sentence could go.

.... a. Don't forget to buy your favorite kind to bring home for dinner!
.... b. Did you know that it wasn't popular in Europe until the nineteenth century?
.... c. The museum also features coins, jewelry, and pieces of rare art.
.... d. There are some museums that try to be a little different.

C *Pair work* Which of these museums would you most like to visit? Why?

12 It could happen to you!

1 SNAPSHOT

Success Stories

Michael Jeffrey Jordan **Born:** February 17, 1963, in Brooklyn, New York **Education:** B.A. from the University of North Carolina	**Madonna Louise Veronica Ciccone** **Born:** August 16, 1958, in Bay City, Michigan **Education:** Two years at the University of Michigan	**William Henry Gates III** **Born:** October 28, 1955, in Seattle, Washington **Education:** Harvard University dropout
Accomplishments: • Generally considered the greatest basketball player of all time • Star of three films and author of two books	**Accomplishments:** • One of the most successful artists in the history of pop music • Won a Golden Globe award for her role in *Evita*	**Accomplishments:** • At 19, founded Microsoft Corporation, the world's leading software company • At 31, became the world's youngest billionaire

Sources: *www.biography.com; www.people.com*

What else do you know about these people?
Which is the most impressive accomplishment of each person?
Name three successful people from your country. What have they accomplished?

2 PERSPECTIVES *It happened to me!*

A  Listen to what happened to these people. Check (✓) the things that have happened to you.

☐ "I was watching a really good movie, but I fell asleep before the end."

☐ "I was working at a boring job when someone offered me a much better one."

☐ "While I was shopping one day, a celebrity walked into the store."

☐ "I was traveling in another country when I met an old school friend."

☐ "While I was waiting in line, a TV reporter asked to interview me for the news!"

☐ "I was getting off a bus when I slipped and fell in some mud."

☐ "While I was walking down the street, I found a wallet full of money."

B Look at the statements again. Which events are lucky? Which are unlucky?

"I hate to fall asleep during a good movie. That's definitely unlucky!"

78

3 GRAMMAR FOCUS

Past continuous vs. simple past ▶

Use the past continuous for an action in progress in the past.
Use the simple past for a completed action.

I **was watching** a good movie,	but I **fell** asleep before the end.
I **was working** at a boring job	when someone **offered** me a much better one.
While I **was shopping** one day,	a celebrity **walked** into the store.

A Complete these sentences. Then compare with a partner.

1. My brother .... (snowboard) when he .... (break) his leg in several places.
2. Several years ago, I .... (have) problems with math, so I .... (find) a tutor to help me.
3. The couple .... (have) their first child when they .... (live) in a tiny apartment.
4. While I .... (drive) in Ireland a few years ago, I .... (realize) I was on the wrong side of the road!
5. Ulrike .... (read) a good book, but someone .... (tell) her the ending.
6. While my mother .... (cook) dinner last night, the phone .... (ring) three times and then .... (stop).
7. Tracy and Eric .... (meet) when they .... (work) at the same restaurant in Vancouver.

B Complete these statements with interesting information about yourself. Use the simple past or the past continuous.

1. During my childhood, . . .
2. When I was going to elementary school, . . .
3. I met my best friend while . . .
4. Two years ago, . . .
5. Last month, . . .

C *Pair work* Take turns reading your sentences from part B. Then ask and answer follow-up questions.

A: During my childhood, my family was living in Chile.
B: Oh, really? That's interesting. What were they doing there?
A: My father was working for a mining company.

4 LISTENING Lucky breaks

A 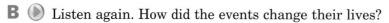 Listen to these stories about lucky breaks. What were the people doing before they got their lucky breaks? What was their lucky break?

	What they were doing	Lucky break
1. Yang Zhifa	....	....
2. Gwyneth Paltrow	....	....

B Listen again. How did the events change their lives?

Terracotta Warriors

5 WORD POWER Storytelling

A Some adverbs are often used in storytelling to emphasize that something interesting is about to happen. Which of these adverbs are positive (**P**)? Which are negative (**N**)? Which are neutral (**E**)?

coincidentally	....	strangely	....
fortunately	....	suddenly	....
luckily	....	surprisingly	....
miraculously	....	unexpectedly	....
sadly	....	unfortunately	....

B *Pair work* Complete these statements with adverbs from part A to make up creative sentences.

I was walking down the street when, . . .
It started out as a normal day, but, . . .
We were on our way to the party when, . . .

A: I was walking down the street when, unexpectedly, it started to rain.
B: Or, I was walking down the street when, suddenly, I found twenty dollars!

6 WRITING A short story

A Write a short story about something that happened to you recently. Try to include some of the adverbs from Exercise 5.

> *I was visiting the coast last year when, unexpectedly, I got a chance to go kayaking. Fortunately, it was a perfect day and I was having a great time. The water was calm and I was beginning to feel a little tired when, suddenly, . . .*

B *Group work* Take turns reading your stories. Answer any questions from the group.

7 CONVERSATION *What have you been doing?*

A ▶ Listen and practice.

Pete: Hey, Gina! I haven't seen you in ages. What have you been doing lately?

Gina: Nothing exciting. I've been working two jobs for the last six months.

Pete: How come?

Gina: I'm saving up money for a trip to Morocco.

Pete: Well, that's exciting.

Gina: Yeah, it is. What about you?

Pete: Well, I've only been *spending* money. I'm pursuing a full-time modeling career.

Gina: Really? How long have you been modeling?

Pete: Since I graduated. But I haven't been getting any work. I need a job soon. I'm almost out of money!

B ▶ Listen to two other people at the party. What has happened since they last saw each other?

8 GRAMMAR FOCUS

Present perfect continuous ▶

Use the present perfect continuous for actions that start in the past and continue into the present.

What **have** you **been doing** lately?	I**'ve been working** two jobs for the last six months.
How long **have** you **been modeling**?	I**'ve been modeling** since I graduated.
Have you **been saving** money?	No, I **haven't been saving** any money. I**'ve been spending** it!

A Complete the conversations with the present perfect continuous. Then practice with a partner.

1. A: What .... you .... (do) lately?
   B: Well, I .... (spend) my free time at the beach.

2. A: .... you .... (work) part time this year?
   B: Yes, I have. I .... (make) drinks at Coffee Time for the past few months.

3. A: How .... you .... (feel) recently?
   B: Great! I .... (get) a lot of sleep. And I .... (not eat) as much since I started my diet.

4. A: .... you .... (get) enough exercise lately?
   B: No, I haven't. I .... (study) a lot for a big exam.

B *Pair work* Take turns asking the questions in part A. Give your own information.

It could happen to you! • **81**

9 PRONUNCIATION Contrastive stress in responses

A ▶ Listen and practice. Notice how the stress changes to emphasize a contrast.

A: Has your brother been studying German?

B: No, I've been studying German.

A: Have you been teaching French?

B: No, I've been studying French.

B ▶ Mark the stress changes in these conversations. Listen and check. Then practice the conversations.

A: Have you been studying for ten years?

B: No, I've been studying for two years.

A: Have you been studying at school?

B: No, I've been studying at home.

10 SPEAKING Tell me about it.

Group work Add four questions to this list. Then take turns asking and answering the questions. Remember to ask for further information.

Have you been . . . lately?

taking driving lessons
working out
learning a new hobby
working long hours
reading any interesting books
doing anything unusual
traveling
dating anyone

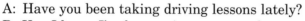

useful expressions
Really? I didn't know that! Oh, I see. Gee, I had no idea. Wow! Tell me more.

A: Have you been taking driving lessons lately?
B: Yes, I have. I've been going every week.
C: How have the lessons been going?
B: Great! I think I'm becoming an excellent driver.

11 INTERCHANGE 12 Life is like a game!

Play a board game. Go to Interchange 12.

CHILD Prodigies

Look at the pictures and skim the article. Which child do you think is an artist? a musician? a college graduate?

Other musicians have described Sarah Chang as "the most wonderful, perfect violinist" they've ever heard. What makes this praise especially surprising is Sarah's age. She's only in her twenties, and people have been describing her this way since she was a child. On Sarah's fourth birthday, her father gave her a violin. By age 5, she was accepted at the famous Juilliard School of Music in New York City. By 8, she was performing as a violin soloist with major orchestras. Since then, Sarah has performed around the world and recorded many albums.

Before Michael Kearney was born, the doctors warned his parents that he might have learning difficulties. He's been proving them wrong ever since! By the time he was 4 months old, Michael could say full sentences like, "What's for dinner, Mom?" By 10 months, he could read words. Studying at home with his parents, Michael completed four grade levels each year. At 10, he graduated from college with honors. And at 14, he received a Master's degree. Now in his late teens, he is teaching and working on his Ph.D.

When Alexandra Nechita was 2, her parents gave her some crayons and coloring books. Alexandra was soon working in inks, watercolors, and by the time she was 7, oil paints. At 8, Alexandra had her first art exhibit. Now a young adult, Alexandra is one of the most recognized artists in the world. Her paintings are often compared to those of Picasso and other great artists. They have sold for as much as $80,000. She has been on TV many times, and several books of her paintings have been published.

A Read the article. Then answer these questions.

1. How do other musicians describe Sarah? ....
2. Who gave Sarah her first violin? ....
3. Where did Sarah go to school? ....
4. What did doctors tell Michael's parents? ....
5. What is Michael doing now? ....
6. What materials has Alexandra worked with? ....
7. What happened to Alexandra when she was 8? ....
8. Whose work has Alexandra's been compared to? ....

B *Pair work* Which of the three prodigies do you think is the most amazing?
If you were a prodigy, what would you like to be really good at? Why?

Units 11-12 Progress check

SELF-ASSESSMENT

How well can you do these things? Check (✓) the boxes.

I can	Very well	OK	A little
Describe accomplishments using the passive with *by* (Ex. 1)	☐	☐	☐
Listen to and understand facts using the passive with and without *by* (Ex. 2)	☐	☐	☐
Describe situations using the passive without *by* (Ex. 3)	☐	☐	☐
Ask and answer questions using the past continuous and the simple past (Ex. 4, 5)	☐	☐	☐
Ask and answer questions using the past perfect continuous (Ex. 5)	☐	☐	☐

1 SPEAKING *Right or wrong?*

A List six novels, movies, songs, albums, or other popular works.
Then write one *who* question for each thing.

> The Matrix movies
> Who played Neo in the Matrix movies?

B *Pair work* Take turns asking your questions.
Use the passive with *by* to answer.

A: Who played Neo in the *Matrix* movies?
B: I think Neo was played by Keanu Reeves.

2 LISTENING *Facts about Spain*

A ▶ Listen to people on a game show answer questions about Spain.
What are the answers? Complete the chart.

1. Currency	....	**4.** A popular sport	....
2. Bordering countries	....	**5.** Two main crops	....
3. Capital	....	**6.** Two industries	....

B ▶ Listen again. Keep score. How much money does each contestant have?

GAME *Sentence-making competition*

Group work Use the passive to write results for these situations.
Then compare with the class. Which group wrote the most sentences?

| Your roommate cleaned the apartment. | There was a big storm yesterday. | Someone broke into your house last night. |

> *The dishes were done.*   *The airport was closed.*   *The window was broken.*

 ROLE PLAY *Alibis*

A famous painting has been stolen from a local museum. It disappeared sometime last Sunday afternoon between 12 P.M. and 4 P.M.

Student A: Student B suspects you stole the painting. Make up an alibi. Take notes on what you were doing that day. Then answer Student B's questions.

Student B: You are a police detective. You think Student A stole the painting. Add two questions to the notebook. Then ask Student A the questions.

Change roles and try the role play again.

Where were you last Sunday?

Did you eat lunch? Who was with you?

What were you wearing that day?

What were you doing between 12 P.M. and 4 P.M.?

Was anyone with you?

....

....

 DISCUSSION *Really? How interesting.*

A *Group work* What interesting things can you find out about your classmates? Ask these questions and others of your own.

Have you been doing anything exciting recently?
Are you studying anything right now?
　How long have you been studying it?
Have you met anyone interesting lately?
Who is your best friend? How did you meet?
Where were you living ten years ago? Did you
　like it there? What do you remember about it?

useful expressions
Really? I didn't know that!
Oh, I see.
Gee, I had no idea.
Wow! Tell me more.

B *Class activity* Tell the class the most interesting thing you learned.

WHAT'S NEXT?

Look at your Self-assessment again. Do you need to review anything?

13 Good book, terrible movie!

1 SNAPSHOT

Movie Mania
Successful movies in their categories:

Movie Type	Film Title
Drama	☐ Titanic
Science Fiction	☐ Star Wars
Horror	☐ Jurassic Park
Fantasy	☐ The Lord of the Rings: The Two Towers
War	☐ Saving Private Ryan
Comedy	☐ Home Alone
Animated	☐ The Lion King
Action	☐ Spider-Man

Source: www.the-movie-times.com

Check (✓) the movies you have seen. Did you enjoy them?
Which type of movie is your favorite? Why?
What are the three best movies you've seen in the past few years?

2 CONVERSATION *What's playing?*

A ▶ Listen and practice.

Roger: Do you want to see a movie tonight?
Carol: Hmm. Maybe. What's playing?
Roger: How about the new James Bond film? I hear it's really exciting.
Carol: Actually, the last one was boring.
Roger: What about the movie based on Stephen King's new novel?
Carol: I don't know. His books are usually fascinating, but I don't like horror movies.
Roger: Well, what do you want to see?
Carol: I'm interested in the new Halle Berry movie. It looks good.
Roger: That's fine with me. She's a wonderful actress.

B ▶ Listen to the rest of the conversation. What happens next? What do they decide to do?

Halle Berry

3 GRAMMAR FOCUS

Participles as adjectives ▶

Present participles
Stephen King's books are **fascinating**.
The last James Bond film was **boring**.
The new Halle Berry movie sounds **interesting**.

Past participles
I'm **fascinated** by Stephen King's books.
I was **bored** by the last James Bond film.
I'm **interested** in the new Halle Berry movie.

A Complete these sentences. Then compare with a partner.

Johnny Depp

1. Johnny Depp is a very .... actor.   (amaze)
2. I find animated films ....   (amuse)
3. I'm not .... in science fiction movies.   (interest)
4. I'm .... by watching television.   (bore)
5. I thought *Jurassic Park* was an .... book.   (excite)
6. I'm .... by J.R.R. Tolkien's novels.   (fascinate)
7. It's .... that horror movies are so popular.   (surprise)

B *Pair work* Complete the description below with the correct form of these words.

| amaze | annoy | confuse | disgust | embarrass | shock |

I had a terrible time at the movies. First, my ticket cost $10. I was really
.... by the price. By mistake, I gave the cashier a $5 bill instead of
a ten. I was a little .... Then there was trash all over the theater.
The mess was .... The people behind me talked during the movie,
which was .... The story was hard to follow. I always find thrillers
too .... I liked the special effects, though. They were .... !

4 WORD POWER Opinions

A Complete the chart with synonyms from the list.

absurd	dumb	marvelous	silly
bizarre	fabulous	odd	terrible
disgusting	fantastic	outstanding	unusual
dreadful	horrible	ridiculous	weird

Awful	Wonderful	Stupid	Strange
....	....	....	....
....	....	....	....
....	....	....	....
....	....	....	....

B Write six sentences like the ones in part A of Exercise 3 about
movies, actors, or novels. Then compare with a partner.

5 LISTENING *How did you like it?*

A ▶ Listen to people talk about books and movies. Do you think each person would recommend the book or movie?

B ▶ Listen again. Check (✓) the adjective that best describes what they say about each one.

1. ☐ fascinating	**2.** ☐ wonderful	**3.** ☐ boring	**4.** ☐ ridiculous
☐ silly	☐ odd	☐ terrific	☐ interesting
☐ strange	☐ boring	☐ dreadful	☐ exciting

6 PRONUNCIATION *Emphatic stress*

A ▶ Listen and practice. Notice how stress and a higher pitch are used to express strong opinions.

That's fascinating!   He was amazing!   Oh, that's terrible!

B *Pair work* Write four statements using these words. Then take turns reading them. Pay attention to emphatic stress.

dreadful   fantastic   horrible   ridiculous

7 DISCUSSION *Let's go to the movies!*

A *Pair work* Take turns asking and answering these questions and others of your own.

What kinds of movies are you interested in? Why?
What kinds of movies do you find boring?
Who are your favorite actors and actresses? Why?
Are there actors or actresses you don't like?
What's the worst movie you have ever seen?
What are your three favorite movies in
    English? Why?
Are there any outstanding movies playing now?

A: What kinds of movies are you interested in?
B: I love action movies.
A: Really? Why is that?
B: They're exciting! What about you?
A: I think action movies are kind of silly. I prefer . . .

B *Group work* Compare your information. Whose taste in movies is most like yours?

8 PERSPECTIVES It's about . . .

A Listen to these people talk about some of their Hollywood favorites. Can you guess what movie or actor each person is describing?

> "I can't believe I saw it nine times! It's a movie that stars Kate Winslet. It's about an ocean liner which hits an iceberg and sinks."

> "He's the actor who won an Academy Award two years in a row. He got the first Oscar for *Philadelphia*, and then he won again the very next year for *Forrest Gump*."

> "I love this movie! It's a comedy about a boy that gets left behind when his family goes on vacation. And there are some burglars who try to break into the house. It's hilarious!"

B Now listen and check your answers.

9 GRAMMAR FOCUS

Relative clauses

Use who or that for people.

He's an actor. He won two Oscars.
He's an actor **who/that** won two Oscars.

Use which or that for things.

It's a movie. It stars Kate Winslet.
It's a movie **which/that** stars Kate Winslet.

A Rewrite B's answers using relative clauses. Then practice with a partner.

1. A: Who is Ang Lee?
   B: He's a movie director. He made the film *Hulk*.

2. A: Have you heard of *Pirates of the Caribbean*?
   B: Yes, it's an action movie. It stars Johnny Depp.

3. A: What's *Chicago*?
   B: It's a musical about a girl. She becomes a celebrity.

4. A: Did you enjoy John Grisham's latest novel?
   B: Yes! It was a great book. It was hard to put down.

B *Pair work* Complete these sentences with relative clauses. Then compare your information around the class.

1. Brad Pitt is an actor . . .   3. Sting is a musician . . .
2. *Gladiator* is a movie . . .   4. *The Simpsons* is a TV show . . .

C *Group work* Choose an actor, movie, musician, or TV show you *don't* like. Others agree or disagree.

10 INTERCHANGE 13 Famous faces

What do you know about movies and TV shows? Go to Interchange 13.

11 SPEAKING Scriptwriters

A *Group work* You are scriptwriters for a television studio. You have to write a new script for a TV detective show or mystery. Plan an interesting story. Make brief notes.

Where does the story take place?
Who are the main characters?
What are the main events?
How does the story end?

B *Class activity* Tell the class about your story.

"Our story is about two secret agents who are chasing after an alien from another planet. There are two main characters. . . . "

12 LISTENING A night at the movies

A ▶ Listen to two critics talk about a new movie. What do they like or not like about it? Rate each item in the chart from 1 to 3.

	Acting	Story	Photography	Special effects
Pauline	....	....	....	....
Colin	....	....	....	....

Ratings
1 = didn't like it
2 = OK
3 = liked it very much

B ▶ Look at the chart in part A. Guess how many stars each critic gave the movie. Then listen to the critics give their ratings.

★ poor   ★★ fair   ★★★ very good   ★★★★ excellent

13 WRITING A movie review

A *Pair work* Choose a movie you both have seen recently and discuss it. Then write a review of it.

What was the movie about?
What did you like about it?
What did you *not* like about it?
How was the acting?
How would you rate it?

B *Class activity* Read your review to the class. Who else has seen the movie? Do they agree with your review?

We recently saw the movie *Chocolat*. It's a comedy about a mysterious woman who moves to a small French village. She opens up a shop that sells delicious chocolates. The acting is very good. The town mayor is an especially funny character who . . .

The Magic of Potter

Scan the article. Where was author J.K. Rowling when she got the idea for Harry Potter?

1   There was a time when no one knew the name Harry Potter. Now the adventures of this extraordinary student at Hogwarts School of Witchcraft and Wizardry are read in over 45 languages, including Russian, Thai, and even ancient Greek. No one can explain the Harry Potter phenomenon – not even J.K. Rowling, his creator.

2   J.K. Rowling was born in England in 1965. From a young age, she knew she wanted to be a writer. When she was 6, she wrote her first story – about a rabbit that gets sick. At school, she used to make up stories to tell her friends.

3   After graduating from college, she worked as a secretary. But she didn't give up her dream. She spent her lunch hour writing stories, mainly for adults. Then in 1990, on a train trip to London, she got the idea for the boy wizard. She says he just appeared in her head. She soon created a whole cast of unique characters to help Harry battle the forces of darkness.

4   She kept working on the story while she was teaching English in Portugal, where she married, had her first child, and divorced a year later. When she returned to England, she brought back a suitcase of Harry Potter stories.

5   After returning home, she was broke and living in a small, cramped apartment. She continued writing, and in 1995, finished the first book in the series, *Harry Potter and the Sorcerer's Stone*. It was published in 1997 and became an unexpected bestseller.

6   Rowling's life has changed dramatically. She has become internationally famous and now earns around $40 million a year. She remarried, had a second child, and currently lives in Scotland.

A Read the article. Then number these sentences from 1 (first event) to 10 (last event).

.... a. She completed her first book.
.... b. She finished school.
.... c. She worked as a secretary.
.... d. Her second child was born.
.... e. She got married for the first time.
.... f. She moved to Portugal.
.... g. She had no money.
.... h. She made up her first story.
.... i. The first Harry Potter book was published.
.... j. She got the idea for Harry Potter.

B Where do these sentences belong? Write the number of the paragraph where each sentence could go.

.... a. She hated going to school, but always loved to read.
.... b. When asked about this popularity, she has said, "I really wrote it for myself."
.... c. There were times when she couldn't even afford to eat.
.... d. Despite her fame and fortune, she's been able to keep her private life.
.... e. She didn't have a pen or paper with her, so she had to memorize it.
.... f. It was filled with ten versions of the first chapter of the book!

C *Pair work* Have you ever read a Harry Potter book? What else do you know about this famous character?

14 So that's what it means!

1 SNAPSHOT

BODY Language

Leave me alone!   That's finished.   I'm thinking.   I don't know.   I'm bored.

Source: *Bodytalk*

Do people in your country use these gestures? Do you?
What other gestures can you use to communicate these meanings?
What are three other gestures you sometimes use? What do they mean?

2 WORD POWER Feelings and gestures

A What is this man doing in each picture? Match each expression with a picture. Then compare with a partner.

1. He's biting his nails. ....
2. He's rolling his eyes. ....
3. He's scratching his head. ....
4. He's tapping his foot. ....
5. He's twirling his hair. ....
6. He's wrinkling his nose. ....

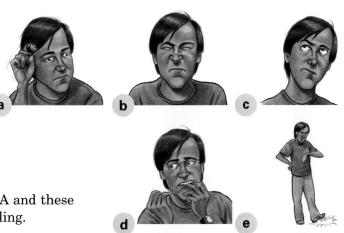

B *Group work* Use the pictures in part A and these adjectives to describe how the man is feeling.

annoyed	confused	embarrassed	frustrated	irritated
bored	disgusted	exhausted	impatient	nervous

"In the first picture, he's twirling his hair. He looks nervous."

92

3 CONVERSATION *Have you met Raj?*

A ▶ Listen and practice.

Ron: Have you met Raj, the student from India?
Emily: No, I haven't.
Ron: Well, he seems really nice, but there's one thing I noticed. He moves his head from side to side when you talk to him. You know, like this.
Emily: Maybe it means he doesn't understand you.
Ron: No, I don't think so.
Emily: Or it could mean he doesn't agree with you.
Peter: Actually, people from India sometimes move their heads from side to side when they agree with you.
Ron: Oh, so that's what it means!

B ▶ Now listen to Raj talk to his friend. What does he find unusual about the way people in North America communicate?

4 GRAMMAR FOCUS

Modals and adverbs ▶

Modals
It **might/may** mean he doesn't understand you.
It **could** mean he doesn't agree with you.
That **must** mean he agrees with you.

Adverbs
Maybe/Perhaps it means he doesn't understand you.
It **possibly/probably** means he doesn't agree with you.
That **definitely** means he agrees with you.

Pair work What do these gestures mean? Take turns making statements about each gesture using the meanings in the box.

possible meanings

Good luck!
Be quiet.
Peace.
That sounds crazy!
I can't hear you.
Come here.

A: What do you think the first gesture means?
B: It probably means . . . , or it might mean . . .

5 SPEAKING *What does it mean?*

A Imagine you are in a foreign country and you don't speak the language. Think of gestures to communicate these meanings.

Go away.	I don't understand.
Help!	It's delicious.
Please repeat.	How much does this cost?
I'm lost.	Someone stole my wallet.
I'm hungry.	Where's the bathroom?

B *Pair work* Take turns acting out your gestures. Can your partner guess what you are trying to say?

C *Group work* What else could your gestures mean? For each gesture you acted out in part B, think of one more possible meaning.

A: This probably means "go away," but it might also mean you don't like something.
B: It could also mean . . .

6 PRONUNCIATION *Pitch*

A Listen and practice. Notice how pitch is used to express certainty or doubt.

	Resolved	*Unresolved*
A: Do you think her gesture means "go away"?	B: Definitely.	B: Probably.
A: Do you understand what her gesture means?	B: Absolutely.	B: Maybe.

B *Pair work* Take turns asking yes/no questions. Respond by using *absolutely*, *definitely*, *maybe*, *probably*, and your own information. Pay attention to pitch.

7 INTERCHANGE 14 *What's going on?*

Interpret people's body language. Go to Interchange 14.

8 PERSPECTIVES *Signs*

A What do you think these international signs mean? Listen and match each sign with the correct meaning.

....

a. You can camp here.
b. You aren't allowed to take photographs here.
c. You have to fasten your seat belts.
d. You can recycle this item.

e. You have to wear a hard hat to enter this area.
f. You can't drink the water here. It's not safe.
g. You have to have your dog on a leash here.
h. You've got to take off your shoes here.

B *Pair work* Where might you see the signs in part A? Give two suggestions for each one.

"You might see this one at a national park or . . ."

9 GRAMMAR FOCUS

Permission, obligation, and prohibition

Permission	**Obligation**	**Prohibition**
You **can** camp here.	You **have to** camp here.	You **can't** camp here.
You**'re allowed to** take off your shoes.	You**'ve got to** take off your shoes.	You **aren't allowed to** take off your shoes.

A Match these school rules with the correct sign. Then compare with a partner.

1. Lock your bikes in the bike rack. ....
2. No eating or drinking in the classroom. ....
3. No playing ball in the hallway. ....
4. Keep the classroom door closed. ....
5. No pets allowed on campus. ....
6. Throw all trash in the wastepaper basket. ....
7. Don't open the windows. ....
8. Turn out the lights when leaving. ....

a · b · c · d

e · f · g · h

B *Pair work* Use the language in the grammar box to take turns talking about each sign.

A: This first sign means you aren't allowed to eat or drink in the classroom.
B: Yes, I think you're right. And the second one means you have to . . .

10 DISCUSSION *Rules and regulations*

A *Pair work* How many rules can you think of for each of these places?

on an airplane	in an art museum	at a zoo
in a library	in a movie theater	at work

"On an airplane, you have to wear your seat belt when the plane is taking off and landing."

> **useful expressions**
>
> You can/can't . . .
> You are/aren't allowed to . . .
> You have to . . .

B *Group work* Share your ideas. Why do you think these rules exist? Have you ever broken any of them? What happened?

11 LISTENING *What's in a sign?*

A ▶ Listen to three conversations about driving. Check (✓) True or False for each statement.

	True	False
1. The man hasn't had a parking ticket lately.	☐	☐
Parking isn't allowed there during working hours.	☐	☐
The fine for parking is $16.	☐	☐
2. The woman is driving faster than the speed limit.	☐	☐
There are other cars in her lane.	☐	☐
The lane is reserved for buses and taxis.	☐	☐
3. The other drivers are flashing their lights.	☐	☐
He's driving with his lights on.	☐	☐
The other drivers are giving him a warning.	☐	☐

B ▶ Listen again. Which drivers did something wrong?

12 WRITING *A list of rules*

A Write a list of rules and regulations for your school or classroom.

B *Group work* Share your lists. Then choose the ten best rules. Work together to write brief explanations of why each is necessary.

> | You aren't allowed to |
> |---|
> | chew gum in class. |

> 1. You aren't allowed to chew gum in class because it may bother other students.
>
> 2. You can keep a library book for only two weeks because someone else might want to check it out.
>
> 3. You have to leave the building to use your cell phone because . . .

Pearls of Wisdom

Look at these proverbs and the pictures below. Then match each proverb with a picture.

> A bird in the hand is worth two in the bush.
> One person's meat is another one's poison.

> Don't count your chickens before they hatch.
> Money doesn't grow on trees.

1 **Why do people use proverbs?** Many people love proverbs for their wisdom. Others enjoy the images in proverbs. But proverbs are most impressive because they express a lot of information in just a few words. A good proverb quickly sums up ideas that are sometimes hard to express. And the person listening immediately understands it.

2 **Where do proverbs come from?** Proverbs come from two main places – ordinary people and famous people. These two sources are not always distinct. Common and popular wisdom has often been used by famous people.

And something said or written down by a well-known person has often been borrowed by the common man. For example, *"Bad news travels fast"* probably comes from the experience of housewives. However, *"All's well that ends well"* was written by William Shakespeare.

3 **What do proverbs tell us?** Proverbs are used everywhere in the world. If you can understand a culture's proverbs, you can better understand the culture itself. There are many different ways that we use proverbs in daily life. Here are some examples. Proverbs can:

Give advice
Meaning: Something you have is better than something you might get.

Give a warning
Meaning: Don't plan on a successful outcome until it actually happens.

Teach a lesson
Meaning: It's not easy to get money.

Express a common truth
Meaning: What one person loves, another person may hate.

A Read the article. Then find these sentences in the article. Decide whether each sentence is the main idea or a supporting idea in that paragraph. Check (✓) the correct boxes.

	Main idea	Supporting idea
1. Many people love proverbs for their wisdom. (par. 1)	☐	☐
2. But proverbs are most . . . just a few words. (par. 1)	☐	☐
3. Proverbs come from . . . and famous people. (par. 2)	☐	☐
4. If you can understand . . . the culture itself. (par. 3)	☐	☐
5. There are many . . . proverbs in daily life. (par. 3)	☐	☐

B *Class activity* Can you think of an interesting proverb from your country? What does it mean? Tell it to the class in English.

Units 13–14 Progress check

SELF-ASSESSMENT

How well can you do these things? Check (✓) the boxes.

I can	Very well	OK	A little
Ask for and give opinions using participles as adjectives (Ex. 1)	☐	☐	☐
Describe people and things using relative clauses (Ex. 2)	☐	☐	☐
Listen to and understand interpretations using modals and adverbs (Ex. 3)	☐	☐	☐
Explain gestures and meanings using modals and adverbs (Ex. 4)	☐	☐	☐
Talk about laws using terms of permission, obligation, and prohibition (Ex. 5)	☐	☐	☐

1 SURVEY Entertainment opinions

A Complete the first column of the survey with your opinions.

	Me	My classmate
A confusing movie	....	....
A boring TV show	....	....
A shocking news story	....	....
A fascinating book	....	....
An interesting celebrity	....	....
A singer you are amazed by	....	....
A song you are annoyed by	....	....

B *Class activity* Go around the class and find someone who has the same opinions. Write a classmate's name only once.

2 ROLE PLAY Movie recommendations

Student A: Invite Student B to a movie. Suggest two films.
Then answer your partner's questions.
Start like this: *Do you want to see a movie?*

Student B: Student A invites you to a movie. Find out more
about the two movies. Then accept or refuse
the invitation.

Change roles and try the role play again.

3 LISTENING *That's how I feel!*

A Listen to some people talking. Write what each person is talking about.

1. ....   2. ....   3. ....   4. ....

B Listen again. What does each person mean? Check (✓) the best answer.

1. ☐ He is confused.
    ☐ He is nervous.

2. ☐ She enjoyed it.
    ☐ She hated it.

3. ☐ He didn't understand it.
    ☐ He thought it was interesting.

4. ☐ She is frustrated.
    ☐ She is bored.

4 GAME *Charades*

A Think of two emotions or ideas you can communicate with gestures. Write them on separate cards.

> I'm tired of waiting.

B *Group work* Shuffle your cards together. Then take turns picking cards and acting out the meanings with gestures. The student who guesses correctly goes next.

A: That probably means you're bored.
B: No.
C: It could mean you're impatient.
B: You're getting closer . . . .

THUMP! THUMP! THUMP!

5 DISCUSSION *What's the law?*

Group work Read these laws from the United States. What do you think about them? Are they the same or different in your country?

- You're allowed to vote when you turn 18.
- In some states, you can get married when you're 16.
- You have to wear a seat belt in the front seat of a car.
- Young men don't have to serve in the military.
- You aren't allowed to keep certain wild animals as pets.
- In some states, you can't drive faster than 65 miles an hour.
- You have to have a passport to enter the country.

A: In the U.S., you're allowed to vote when you turn 18.
B: That's surprising! In my country, we *have* to vote when we're 18.
C: And in my country, we *can't* vote until we're 20.

WHAT'S NEXT?

Look at your Self-assessment again. Do you need to review anything?

15 What would you do?

SNAPSHOT

STORIES OF HONESTY

BUSINESSMAN RETURNS $750,000 TO OWNER	*Fan Returns Soccer Star's Lucky T-shirt:*	Student Uses Detective Work	Athlete Admits to Cheating
and is thanked with a brief phone call.	Player meets him to personally give $1,000 reward.	to find owner of gold jewelry. "I thought it might have personal value," he told reporters.	"I'm so sorry. I just wanted to win," he recently confessed. "I feel so ashamed."

Source: *The Los Angeles Times*

Do you know any other stories like these?
Have you ever found anything valuable? What did you do?
Do you think that people who return lost things should get a reward?

2 **CONVERSATION** *If I found $750,000 . . .*

A ▶ Listen and practice.

Phil: Look at this. Some guy found $750,000!
      He returned it and the owner simply
      thanked him with a phone call.
 Pat: You're kidding! If I found $750,000,
      I wouldn't return it so fast.
Phil: Why? What would you do?
 Pat: Well, I'd go straight to the mall and spend
      it. I could buy lots of nice clothes and jewelry.
Phil: Someone might also find out about it.
      And then you could go to jail.
 Pat: Hmm. You've got a point there.

B ▶ Listen to the rest of the conversation.
What would Phil do if he found $750,000?

3 GRAMMAR FOCUS

Unreal conditional sentences with if clauses ▶

Unreal conditional sentences describe imaginary situations with simple past forms and consequences in the present.

What **would** you **do if** you **found** $750,000?

If I **found** $750,000,

I **would**/I'**d go** straight to the mall.
I **could buy** lots of nice clothes and jewelry.
I **might go** to the police.
I **wouldn't return** it so fast.

A Complete these conversations. Then compare with a partner.

1. A: If you .... (have) three months to travel, where .... you .... (go)?
   B: Oh, that's easy! I .... (fly) to Antarctica. I've always wanted to go there.

2. A: If your doctor .... (tell) you to get more exercise, which sport .... you .... (choose)?
   B: I'm not sure, but I .... (go) jogging two or three times a week.

3. A: What .... you .... (do) if your car .... (break down)?
   B: If I couldn't afford to fix it, I .... (have to) walk everywhere.

4. A: .... you .... (break) into your house if you .... (lock) yourself out?
   B: If I .... (not have) another key, I .... (ask) a neighbor for help.

B *Pair work* Take turns asking and answering questions.

What would you do if . . . ?

you saw a burglar in your home
you found a diamond ring
you saw someone shoplifting
you won a million dollars in a lottery
your teacher gave you an A on a test by mistake
your friend wanted to marry someone you didn't trust

4 LISTENING *Tough predicaments*

A ▶ Listen to three people talk about predicaments. Number them in the order they are discussed.

Predicament	Suggestions
☐ Two people were fighting in the street.	....
☐ A friend lost all her money while traveling.	....
☐ A friend has a serious shopping problem.	....

B ▶ Listen again. What suggestions do the people give for each predicament? Take notes. Which is the best suggestion?

INTERCHANGE 15 *Do the right thing!*

What would you do in some difficult situations? Go to Interchange 15.

6 **WORD POWER** *Antonyms*

A Find nine pairs of opposites in this list. Complete the chart.
Then compare with a partner.

✓ accept	borrow	dislike	find	lose	remember
admit	deny	divorce	forget	marry	save
agree	disagree	enjoy	lend	✓ refuse	spend

accept ≠ *refuse*	.... ≠	.... ≠ ....
.... ≠	.... ≠	.... ≠ ....
.... ≠	.... ≠	.... ≠ ....

B *Pair work* Choose four pairs of opposites. Write sentences using each pair.

> *I can never save money because I spend it all on clothes.*

7 **PERSPECTIVES** *I felt terrible.*

A ▶ Listen to people talk about recent predicaments.
Then check (✓) the best suggestion for each one.

"**What** a disaster! I spilled juice on my parents' new couch. They weren't home, so I just turned the cushions over. What should I have done?"

☐ You should have told them about it.

☐ You should have cleaned it immediately.

☐ You should have offered to buy them a new couch.

"**I** forgot my best friend's birthday. I felt terrible, so I sent him an e-mail to apologize. What would you have done?"

☐ I would have called him right away.

☐ I would have sent him a nice birthday present.

☐ I would have invited him out for a meal.

B *Pair work* Compare with a partner. Do you agree with each other?

8 GRAMMAR FOCUS

Past modals ▶

Use would have or should have + past participle to give opinions or suggestions about actions in the past.

What **should** I **have done**?	You **should have told** them about it.
	You **shouldn't have hidden** it.
What **would** you **have done**?	I **would have called** him.
	I **wouldn't have sent** him an e-mail.

A Complete these conversations. Then practice with a partner.

1. A: The cashier gave me too much change. What should I have .... (do)?
   B: You should have .... (say) something. You shouldn't have .... (take) the money.

2. A: I ignored an e-mail from someone I don't like. What would you have .... (do)?
   B: I would have .... (reply) to the person. It just takes a minute!

3. A: I was watching a good movie when the phone rang. What should I have .... (do)?
   B: You should have .... (take) the call and .... (tell) the person you'd call later.

4. A: We left all our trash at the campsite. What would you have .... (do)?
   B: I would have .... (take) it with me and .... (throw) it away later.

B Read the situations below. What would have been the best thing to do? Choose suggestions. Then compare with a partner.

Situations

1. The teacher borrowed my favorite book and spilled coffee all over it. ....
2. I saw a classmate cheating on an exam. So I wrote her a letter about it. ....
3. A friend of mine always has messy hair. So I gave him a comb for his birthday. ....
4. I hit someone's car when I was leaving a parking lot. Luckily, no one saw me. ....
5. My aunt gave me a wool sweater. I can't wear wool, so I gave it back. ....

Suggestions

a. You should have spoken to him about it.
b. I would have spoken to the teacher about it.
c. I would have waited for the owner to return.
d. I wouldn't have said anything.
e. You should have warned her not to do it again.
f. You should have left a note for the owner.
g. I would have told her that I'd prefer something else.
h. You should have exchanged it for something else.

C *Group work* Make another suggestion for each situation in part B.

9 PRONUNCIATION Reduction of have

A ▶ Listen and practice. Notice how **have** is reduced in these sentences.

/əv/
What would you have done?

/əv/
I would have told the truth.

B *Pair work* Practice the conversations in part A of Exercise 8 again. Use the reduced form of **have**.

10 LISTENING I'm calling about . . .

A ▶ Listen to people calling Dr. Hilda, a counselor on a radio talk show. Complete the chart.

	Problem	What the caller did
Caller 1	....	....
Caller 2	....	....
Caller 3	....	....

B ▶ Listen again. According to Dr. Hilda, what should each caller have done?

C *Group work* Do you agree with Dr. Hilda? What would you have done?

11 SPEAKING I shouldn't have . . .

A Look at the five situations below. Think about the past month and write down an example for each situation.

1. something you shouldn't have bought
2. something you should have done
3. someone you should have called
4. something you shouldn't have said
5. someone you should have e-mailed or written

B *Group work* Talk about each situation in part A.

A: I bought a lamp at a garage sale. I shouldn't have bought it because I don't really like it.
B: I did something similar recently. I shouldn't have bought . . .

12 WRITING A letter to an advice columnist

Write a letter to an advice columnist about a real or imaginary problem. Put your letters on a bulletin board and choose one to write a reply to.

> *Dear Dr. Hilda,*
>   I let a friend borrow my laptop and now it doesn't work. I took it to a repair shop, and they said it would be expensive to fix. When I asked my friend to help me pay the bill, she refused.
>
> Now she won't even speak to me! What did I do wrong? What should I have done?
>
> *Can't Do Anything Right*

Ask Amy

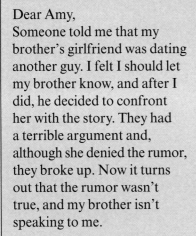

Scan the three letters to Amy. What problems do the writers ask for help with?

Dear Amy,
Someone told me that my brother's girlfriend was dating another guy. I felt I should let my brother know, and after I did, he decided to confront her with the story. They had a terrible argument and, although she denied the rumor, they broke up. Now it turns out that the rumor wasn't true, and my brother isn't speaking to me.

Distraught Sister

Dear Amy,
My son is 23 years old. He finished college last year, but he can't seem to find a job he likes. He still lives at home, and I'm worried that he's not trying hard enough to get a job and support himself. Meanwhile, I've been cooking his meals and doing his laundry.

Tired Mom

Dear Amy,
I went to the movies with my best friend and her younger brother. She wasn't feeling well, so afterward, he drove me home. While we were driving, he told me he had skipped school that day, taken his mother's car, and gone to the beach! My dilemma is: Should I tell my friend about this?

Confused Friend

Dear . . . ,
You should have thought more carefully before you acted. It wasn't necessary to get angry. Next time, speak to the child immediately and warn him not to do it again.

Amy

Dear . . . ,
You're making it too easy for him to stay where he is. Be firm and tell him he has two months to find a job and get his own place. He's old enough to take care of himself – but you have to be willing to let him go.

Amy

Dear . . . ,
I would suggest you keep quiet. Let them work things out for themselves. If you say something, you could damage your friendship with both of them.

Amy

Dear . . . ,
Well, you learned a lesson. You shouldn't have listened to gossip. And you shouldn't have passed it on. Now you have to repair the damage. Apologize sincerely and hope he will forgive and forget.

Amy

A Read the article. Then match the letters with the replies. (There is one extra reply.)

B Find the words in *italics* in the article. Then match each word or phrase with its meaning.

.... 1. *confront*   a. make a fresh start
.... 2. *distraught*   b. find a solution
.... 3. *dilemma*   c. challenge in a direct way
.... 4. *firm*   d. strong and determined
.... 5. *work (things) out*   e. a difficult problem
.... 6. *forgive and forget*   f. extremely worried or upset

C *Pair work* Do you agree with Amy's advice? What advice would you give?
Think of a problem you are having. Ask your partner for advice.

16 What's your excuse?

SNAPSHOT

EXCUSES, EXCUSES

Situation	Excuse
Being late	My watch stopped. My class got out late.
Forgetting to meet someone	I wrote down the wrong date. I forgot to check my calendar.
Not doing homework	My sister was using the computer. I thought it was due tomorrow.
Getting home late	I couldn't get a ride. I missed the bus.
Not accepting a date	I'm not allowed to date. I have a boyfriend/girlfriend.

"I'm sorry I'm late. My watch stopped."

Have you ever heard any of these excuses? Have you ever used any of them?
Which are good excuses? Which are bad excuses?
What other excuses can you make for not accepting an invitation?

2 **PERSPECTIVES** Who said it?

A Who do you think made these requests? Listen and match each
request with a person.

1. He asked me to play my music more quietly. ....
2. She told me not to come home after midnight. ....
3. She said to drink at least six glasses of water a day. ....
4. He said not to be late for practice again. ....
5. She asked me to pick up the kids after school. ....
6. He told me to bring a dictionary tomorrow. ....
7. He asked me not to tell anyone about his new girlfriend. ....

a. my doctor
b. my coach
c. my friend
d. my neighbor
e. my mother
f. my wife
g. my teacher

B *Pair work* Can you think of another request each person
might make?

A: A doctor might also tell a patient to get more exercise.
B: . . . or to avoid eating greasy foods.

3 GRAMMAR FOCUS

Reported speech: requests ▶

Original request

Can you play your music more quietly?

Don't come home after midnight.

Reported request

He **asked me to play** my music more quietly.

She **told me not to come** home after midnight.
She **said not to come** home after midnight.

A Amanda is having a suprise party for Albert. Look at what she told
the guests. Write each request using *ask*, *tell*, or *say*. Then compare
with a partner.

1. Meet at Albert's apartment at 7:30.
2. Can you bring your favorite CDs?
3. Don't bring any food.
4. Can you bring a small gift for Albert?
5. Don't spend more than $10 on the gift.
6. Be careful not to say anything to him.

> Amanda told them to meet at
> Albert's apartment at 7:30.

B *Group work* Imagine you're planning a class party. Write four requests.
Then take turns reading your requests and changing them into reported requests.

Juan: Bring something good to eat to the party!
Sonia: Juan told us to bring something good to eat.

Noriko: Can you help me clean up after the party?
Jin Sook: Noriko asked us to help her clean up.

4 SPEAKING What a request!

A Think of requests that people have made recently.
Write two things people asked you to do and two
things people asked you *not* to do.

Person	Request
my mom	*get a haircut*

B *Group work* Compare with others. Who has the most
interesting or unusual requests? Who did what was asked?

A: My mom asked me to get a haircut.
B: What did you tell her?

5 WORD POWER Verb and noun pairs

A Find three words or phrases in the list that are usually paired with each verb. Then compare with a partner.

anger	a compliment	a criticism	a joke	your regrets
an apology	a concern	an excuse	a lie	sympathy
a complaint	your congratulations	an invitation	a reason	the truth

express	....	....	....
give	....	....	....
make	....	....	....
offer	....	....	....
tell	....	....	....

B *Pair work* In what situations do you do the things in part A?
Write five sentences about things you *never*, *sometimes*, or *always* do.
Then take turns reading your sentences and asking questions.

A: I never tell a lie.
B: Are you sure? What if someone asks how much you weigh?

6 CONVERSATION Are you doing anything on Saturday?

A ▶ Listen and practice.

Albert: Hi, Daniel. This is Albert.
Daniel: Oh, hi. How are things?
Albert: Just fine, thanks. Uh, are you doing anything on Saturday night?
Daniel: Hmm. Saturday night? Let me think. Oh, yes. My cousin just called to say he was flying in that night. I told him I would pick him up.
Albert: Oh, that's too bad! It's my birthday. I'm having dinner with Amanda, and I thought I'd invite more people and make it a party.
Daniel: Gee, I'm really sorry, but I won't be able to make it.
Albert: I'm sorry, too. But that's OK.

B *Pair work* Act out the conversation in part A. Make up your own excuse for not accepting Albert's invitation.

LISTENING *He said, she said*

A  Listen to Albert inviting friends to his party on Saturday.
What excuses do people give for not coming? Match the person to the excuse.

1. Scott ....
2. Fumiko ....
3. Manuel ....
4. Regina ....

a. She said that she wasn't feeling well.
b. He said he was taking his mother to a dance club.
c. She said she had houseguests for the weekend.
d. He said that he would be out of town.
e. She said she might go out with friends.
f. He said he was going away with his family.

B Listen. What happens on the night of Albert's birthday?

8 **GRAMMAR FOCUS**

> **Reported speech: statements**
>
> | **Direct statement** | **Reported statement** | |
> |---|---|---|
> | I'm **not feeling** well. | She **said** (that) | she **wasn't feeling** well. |
> | I **have** houseguests for the weekend. | | she **had** houseguests for the weekend. |
> | I **made** a tennis date with Kim. | | she **had made** a tennis date with Kim. |
> | I **have planned** an exciting trip. | | she **had planned** an exciting trip. |
> | We **can't come** tomorrow. | They **told me** (that) | they **couldn't come** tomorrow. |
> | We **will be** out of town. | | they **would be** out of town. |
> | We **may go** out with friends. | | they **might go** out with friends. |

A Sandra is having a party at her house on Saturday. Look at these excuses.
Change them into reported speech. Then compare with a partner.

1. Donna: "I have to baby-sit my nephew that night."
2. William and Brigitte: "We're going out of town for the weekend."
3. Mary: "I've been invited to a wedding on Saturday."
4. James: "I promised to help Dennis move."
5. Anita: "I can't come because I have the flu."
6. Mark: "I'll be studying for a test all weekend."
7. Eva and Randall: "We have to pick someone up at the airport that evening."
8. David: "I may have to work late on Saturday night."

> *Donna said she had to baby-sit her nephew that night.*
> *Donna told her she had to baby-sit her nephew that night.*

B *Group work* Imagine you don't want to go to Sandra's party. Take turns
making excuses and changing them into reported speech.

A: I'm sorry I can't go. I have tickets to a concert that night.
B: Lucky guy! He said he had tickets to a concert that night.

9 PRONUNCIATION *Reduction of had and would*

A ▶ Listen and practice. Notice how **had** and **would** are reduced in the following sentences.

She said she'd made the bed. (She said she **had made** the bed.)
She said she'd make the bed. (She said she **would make** the bed.)

B ▶ Listen to four sentences. Check (✓) if you hear the reduced form of **had** or **would**.

1. ☐ had   2. ☐ had   3. ☐ had   4. ☐ had
   ☐ would   ☐ would   ☐ would   ☐ would

10 SPEAKING *Good intentions*

A *Group work* What are some things you would like to do in the near future? Think of three intentions.

A: I'm going to learn how to sail.
B: That sounds fun. Are you going to take lessons?

B *Class activity* Report the best intentions you heard. Then predict which ones will happen.

"Tatyana said she was going to learn how to sail, but she doesn't want to take lessons."

11 WRITING *A voice mail message*

A ▶ Dan is out of town for the weekend. Listen to four voice mails he received. His roommate has written down the first message. Write down the three other messages.

Dan— Friday, 9 P.M.
Bill called. He said
he would meet you
in front of Pizza
House at 6:30 P.M.
on Monday.

B *Pair work* Compare your messages. Is any important information missing?

12 INTERCHANGE 16 *Excuses, excuses*

Make some plans. Student A find Interchange 16A; Student B find Interchange 16B.

The Truth About Lying

Is it ever better to tell a lie rather than the truth? If so, when?

Most of us are taught to believe that lying is wrong. But it seems that everybody tells lies – not big lies, but what we call "white lies." If we believe that lying is wrong, why do we do it? Most of the time, people have very good reasons for lying. For example, they might want to protect a friendship or someone's feelings. So, when do we lie and who do we lie to? A recent study found that the average person lies about seven times a day. Here are some ways and reasons why.

#1 Lying to hide something: People often lie because they want to hide something from someone. For example, a son doesn't tell his parents that he's dating a girl because he doesn't think they will like her. Instead, he says he's going out with the guys.

#2 Lying to make an excuse: Sometimes people lie because they don't want to do something. For example, someone invites you to a party. You think it will be boring, so you say you're busy.

#3 Lying to make someone feel good: Often we stretch the truth to make someone feel good. For example, your friend cooks dinner for you, but it tastes terrible. Do you say so? No. You probably say, "Mmm, this is delicious!"

#4 Lying to avoid sharing bad news: Sometimes we don't want to tell someone bad news. For example, you have just had a very bad day at work, but you don't feel like talking about it. So if someone asks you about your day, you just say that everything was fine.

A Read the article. Then complete the summary with information from the article.

It isn't necessarily .... to lie. It's probably OK to lie if you want to protect
.... or .... The main reasons for lying are to .... ,
to .... , to .... , or to ....

B Look at these situations. For each example, write the number of the appropriate reason.

.... 1. Your friend gives you an ugly shirt for your birthday. You say, "Oh, it's great!"
.... 2. You lost your job and are having trouble finding a new one. When an old friend calls to find out how you are, you say you're doing well.
.... 3. Someone you don't like invites you to a movie, so you say, "I've already seen it."
.... 4. You're planning a surprise party for a friend. To get him to come over at the right time, you ask him to stop by to see your new motorcycle.

C *Group work* Can you think of other reasons people tell white lies?
What white lies have you told recently?

Units 15–16 Progress check

SELF-ASSESSMENT

How well can you do these things? Check (✓) the boxes.

I can	Very well	OK	A little
Speculate about imaginary events using unreal conditional sentences (Ex. 1)	☐	☐	☐
Talk about events in the past using past modals (Ex. 2)	☐	☐	☐
Ask for and give opinions or suggestions using past modals (Ex. 2)	☐	☐	☐
Listen to and understand requests (Ex. 3)	☐	☐	☐
Describe what people say and request using reported speech (Ex. 3, 4)	☐	☐	☐

1 DISCUSSION *Interesting situations*

A What would you do in these situations? Complete the statements.

If I found a valuable piece of jewelry in the park, ...
If a friend gave me a present I didn't like, ...
If I wasn't invited to a party I wanted to attend, ...
If a classmate wanted to copy my homework, ...
If someone took my clothes while I was swimming, ...

B *Group work* Compare your suggestions. For each situation, choose one to tell the class.

A: What would you do if you found some jewelry in the park?
B: I'd probably keep it. You'd never be able to find the owner.

2 SPEAKING *Dilemmas*

A Make up two situations like the one below. Think about experiences you have had or heard about at work, home, or school.

"A friend visited me recently. We had a great time at first, but she became annoying. She borrowed my clothes and refused to pay for things. After two weeks, I told her she had to leave because my parents were coming."

B *Pair work* Take turns sharing your situations. Ask for advice and suggestions.

A: What would you have done?
B: Well, I would have told her to leave after three days.

3 LISTENING *Take a message.*

A ▶ Listen to the conversations. Who would make these requests?
Match conversations 1 to 6 to the correct person.

.... a. boss   .... c. neighbor   .... e. classmate
.... b. doctor   .... d. parent   .... f. teacher

B ▶ Listen again. Complete the requests.

1. Please ....   4. Can .... ?
2. Can .... ?   5. Please ....
3. Don't ....   6. Please don't ....

C *Pair work* Work with a partner. Imagine these requests were for you.
Take turns reporting the requests to your partner.

4 GAME *Tell the truth.*

A Think of situations when you *expressed anger, gave an excuse,* or
made a complaint. Write a brief statement about each situation.

> *I once complained about the food in a restaurant.*

B *Class activity* Play a game. Choose three students to be contestants.

Step 1: The contestants compare their statements and choose one. This
statement should be true about only one student. The other two students
should pretend they had the experience.

Step 2: The contestants stand in front of the class. Each contestant
reads the same statement. The rest of the class must ask questions to
find out who isn't telling the truth.

Contestant A, what restaurant were you in?   *Contestant B, what was wrong with the food?*

Contestant C, what did the waiter do?

Step 3: Who isn't telling the truth? What did he or she say to make you think that?

"I don't think Contestant A is telling the truth. He said he couldn't
remember the name of the restaurant!"

WHAT'S NEXT?

Look at your Self-assessment again. Do you need to review anything?

Interchange activities

CLASS PROFILE

A *Class activity* Go around the class and find out the information below. Then ask follow-up questions and take notes. Write a classmate's name only once.

I used to look very different.

Find someone who	Name	Notes
1. used to look very different **"Did you use to look very different?"**	. . . .	. . . .
2. always listened to his or her teachers **"Did you always listen to your teachers?"**	. . . .	. . . .
3. wanted to be a movie star when he or she was younger **"Did you want to be a movie star when you were younger?"**	. . . .	. . . .
4. used to have a favorite toy **"Did you use to have a favorite toy?"**	. . . .	. . . .
5. changed schools when he or she was a child " . . . . ?"	. . . .	. . . .
6. used to fight a lot with his or her brothers and sisters " . . . . ?"	. . . .	. . . .
7. got in trouble a lot as a child " . . . . ?"	. . . .	. . . .
8. had a pet when he or she was little " . . . . ?"	. . . .	. . . .

B *Group work* Tell the group the most interesting thing you learned about your classmates.

TOURISM CAMPAIGN

A *Pair work* Look at the photos and slogans below. What do you think the theme of each tourism campaign is?

possible themes

art	food	nature
culture	history	shopping
entertainment	music	sports

Rio de Janeiro
"Carnaval and Natural Marvels"

Cairo
"The Earth's Mother"

Hong Kong
"A Diner's Paradise"

Café Mozart

Salzburg
"A Musical Banquet"

B *Group work* Imagine you are planning a campaign to attract more tourists to one of the cities above or to a city of your choice. Use the ideas below or your own ideas to discuss the campaign.

best time to visit
famous historical attractions
special events or festivals
nicest area to stay
interesting places to see

A: Do you know when the best time to visit Rio is?
B: Probably in February or March because . . .

C *Group work* What will be the theme of your campaign? What slogan will you use?

WISHFUL THINKING

A Complete this questionnaire with information about yourself.

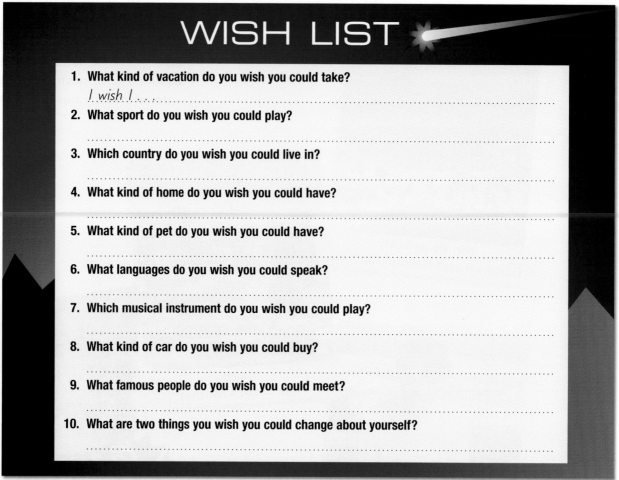

WISH LIST

1. What kind of vacation do you wish you could take?
   I wish I . . . .
2. What sport do you wish you could play?
3. Which country do you wish you could live in?
4. What kind of home do you wish you could have?
5. What kind of pet do you wish you could have?
6. What languages do you wish you could speak?
7. Which musical instrument do you wish you could play?
8. What kind of car do you wish you could buy?
9. What famous people do you wish you could meet?
10. What are two things you wish you could change about yourself?

B *Pair work* Compare your questionnaires. Take turns asking and answering questions about your wishes.

A: What kind of vacation do you wish you could take?
B: I wish I could go on a safari.
A: Really? Why?
B: Well, I could take some great pictures of wild animals!

C *Class activity* Imagine you are at a class reunion. It is ten years since you completed the questionnaire in part A. Tell the class about some wishes that have come true for your partner.

"Sue is a photographer now. She travels to Africa every year and takes pictures of wild animals. Her photos are in many magazines."

A How much do you really know about your classmates? Look at the survey and add two more situations to items 1 and 2.

	Name	Notes
1. Find someone who has		
a. cried during a movie		
b. had food poisoning		
c. been on TV		
d. studied all night for an exam		
e. lied about his or her age		
f.		
g.		
2. Find someone who has never		
a. driven a car		
b. used a recipe to cook		
c. had a cup of coffee		
d. played a video game		
e. eaten pizza		
f.		
g.		

B *Class activity* Go around the class and
ask the questions in the survey. Write
down the names of classmates who answer
"yes" for item 1 and "no" for item 2. Then
ask follow-up questions and take notes.

A: Have you ever cried during a movie?
B: Yes. I've cried during a lot of movies.
A: What kinds of movies?
B: Well, sad ones like *Casablanca* and . . .

A: Have you ever driven a car?
C: No, I haven't.
A: Why not?
C: Well, I'm too young. I don't have a
  driver's license.

C *Group work* Compare the
information in your surveys.

Student A

A *Pair work* You and your partner are going to take a trip. You have a brochure for a ski trip, and your partner has a brochure for a surfing trip.

First, find out about the surfing trip. Ask your partner questions about these things.

the cost of the trip   what the price includes   the accommodations
surfing lessons   entertainment options   the nightlife

B *Pair work* Now use the information in this brochure to answer your partner's questions about the ski trip.

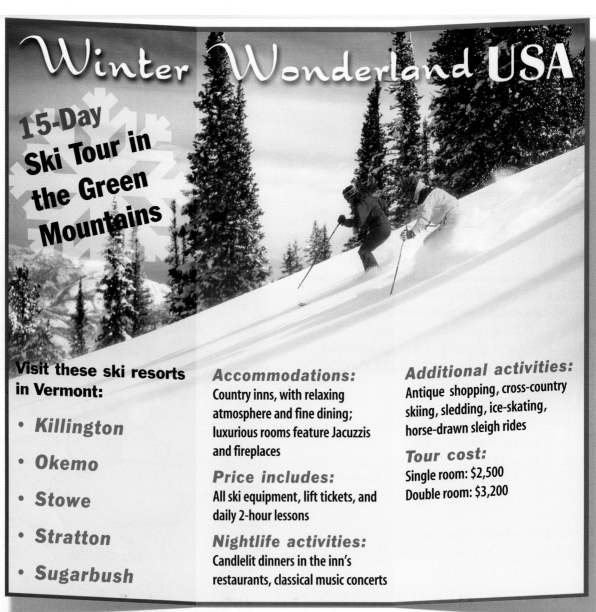

Winter Wonderland USA

15-Day Ski Tour in the Green Mountains

Visit these ski resorts in Vermont:

- **Killington**
- **Okemo**
- **Stowe**
- **Stratton**
- **Sugarbush**

Accommodations:
Country inns, with relaxing atmosphere and fine dining; luxurious rooms feature Jacuzzis and fireplaces

Price includes:
All ski equipment, lift tickets, and daily 2-hour lessons

Nightlife activities:
Candlelit dinners in the inn's restaurants, classical music concerts

Additional activities:
Antique shopping, cross-country skiing, sledding, ice-skating, horse-drawn sleigh rides

Tour cost:
Single room: $2,500
Double room: $3,200

C *Pair work* Decide which trip you are going to take. Then explain your choice to the class.

THAT'S NO EXCUSE!

A *Pair work* Look at these situations and act out conversations. Apologize and then give an excuse, admit a mistake, or make an offer or promise.

1

Student A: You're the customer.
Student B: You're the hairstylist.

A: My hair! You ruined my hair!
B: Oh, I'm so sorry. I . . .

2

Student A: You own the puppy.
Student B: You own the backpack.

3

Student A: You're driving the red car.
Student B: You're driving the blue car.

4

Student A: You're the customer.
Student B: You're the cashier.

B *Group work* Have you ever experienced situations like these? What happened? What did you do? Share your stories.

Student B

A *Pair work* You and your partner are going to take a trip. You have a brochure for a surfing trip, and your partner has a brochure for a ski trip.

First, use the information in this brochure to answer your partner's questions about the surfing trip.

Summer Surfing USA

15-DAY TOUR FOR BEACH LOVERS

Visit these beautiful Southern California surfing beaches:

- **El Capitan in Santa Barbara**
- **Surf Riders in Malibu**
- **The Wedge at Newport Beach**
- **Doheny at Dana Point**

Accommodations:
Single or double rooms in beachfront hotels

Price includes:
Daily surfboard rental, 3-hour beginner's class

Nightlife activities:
Beach barbecues, club dancing, moonlight cruise

Additional activities:
Visit Universal Studios and Disneyland

Tour Beverly Hills and see the movie stars' homes

Tour cost:
Single room: $1,999
Double room: $2,300

B *Pair work* Now find out about the ski trip. Ask your partner questions about these things.

the cost of the trip   what the price includes   the accommodations
ski lessons   entertainment options   the nightlife

C *Pair work* Decide which trip you are going to take. Then explain your choice to the class.

A *Group work* Look at the four problems that people called a radio program about. What advice would you give each caller? Discuss possible suggestions, and then choose the best one.

Caller 1: My family and I are going away on vacation and our house will be empty. How can we make our home safe from burglars?

Caller 2: One of my classmates wants to borrow my new CD player to take with him on vacation. I don't want to lend it to him. What can I say?

Caller 3: I'm going to meet my girlfriend's parents tomorrow for the first time. How can I make a good impression?

Caller 4: Our neighbor's dog barks all night and keeps everybody in the neighborhood awake. What can we do?

B *Pair work* Take turns "calling" a radio station and explaining your problems. Use the situations above or create new ones. Your partner should give you advice.

A: My family and I are going away on vacation and our house will be empty. How can we make our home safe from burglars?

B: Well, don't forget to lock all the windows. Oh, and make sure to . . .

A *Class activity* How do your classmates celebrate special days and times? Go around the class and ask the questions below. If someone answers "yes," write down his or her name. Ask for more information and take notes.

	Name	Notes
1. Does your family have big get-togethers?		
2. Do you ever buy flowers for someone special?		
3. Do you like to watch street parades?		
4. Do you wear your national dress at least once a year?		
5. Has someone given you money recently as a gift?		
6. Have you ever given someone a surprise birthday party?		
7. Do you like to celebrate your birthday with a party?		
8. Do you ever send birthday cards?		
9. Do you ever give friends birthday presents?		
10. Is New Year's your favorite time of the year?		
11. Do you ever celebrate a holiday with fireworks?		

A: Does your family have big get-togethers?
B: Yes, we do.
A: What do you do when you get together?
B: Well, we have a big meal. After we eat, we watch old home movies.

B *Pair work* Compare your information with a partner.

CONSIDER THE CONSEQUENCES

A Read over this questionnaire. Check (✓) the column that states your opinion.

	I agree.	I don't agree.	It depends.
1. If people watch less TV, they'll talk more with their families.	☐	☐	☐
2. If children watch a lot of violent programs on TV, they'll become violent themselves.	☐	☐	☐
3. If people work only four days a week, their lives will improve.	☐	☐	☐
4. If people have smaller families, they'll have better lives.	☐	☐	☐
5. If a woman works outside the home, her children won't be happy.	☐	☐	☐
6. If a woman becomes the leader of a country, a lot of things will change for the better.	☐	☐	☐
7. If cities provide free public transportation, there will be fewer cars on the road and less pollution.	☐	☐	☐
8. If there is a heavy fine for littering, our streets will be much cleaner.	☐	☐	☐
9. If teachers put all their lessons on the Internet, students will learn more.	☐	☐	☐
10. If teachers don't give tests, students won't study.	☐	☐	☐

B *Group work* Compare your opinions. Be prepared to give reasons for your opinions.

A: I think if people watch less TV, they'll talk more with their families.
B: I don't really agree.
C: Why not?
B: Well, if they don't watch TV, they'll do something else. They may read or spend all day on the computer.
C: I agree. Or they might go out and spend *less* time at home with their families.

I think that if they . . .   I agree with you.   I don't agree, because . . .

A Look at the following job descriptions. Choose one that you'd like to apply for.

Marketing Manager

Requirements:
- Must have a business degree or marketing experience
- Must be available to travel and work long hours
- Must enjoy sports and fitness activities

Responsibilities:
- Interviewing people about their sports preferences, writing reports, and working with famous athletes

Personal Assistant

Requirements:
- Must have excellent telephone skills
- Must be willing to work flexible hours
- Must be able to take orders and make important decisions

Responsibilities:
- Maintaining the calendar of a busy celebrity, scheduling meetings, and preparing the star for public appearances

Activities Director

Requirements:
- Must have experience working with tourists
- Must be a "people person"
- Must be outgoing and creative

Responsibilities:
- Organizing all leisure activities on a popular cruise ship, including planning daily excursions, special menus, and nightly entertainment

REGENCY RECRUITERS

B *Pair work* Take turns interviewing each other for the job you each want. Give as much information as you can to show that you are the right person for the job.

C *Pair work* Would you hire your partner for the job? Why or why not?

useful questions

What kind of degree do you have?
What work experience do you have?
What hours can you work?
Do you mind working . . . ?
Are you interested in working with . . . ?
Why should I hire you for the job?

WHO IS THIS BY?

A List one movie, one song, and one CD.

B *Group work* Take turns making a statement about each item. Does everyone agree with each statement?

A: The *Lord of the Rings* movies were filmed in New Zealand.
B: Are you sure? Weren't they filmed in Australia?
C: I'm pretty sure it was New Zealand.

C Now think of other famous creations and creators. Complete the chart. Make some of them true and some of them false.

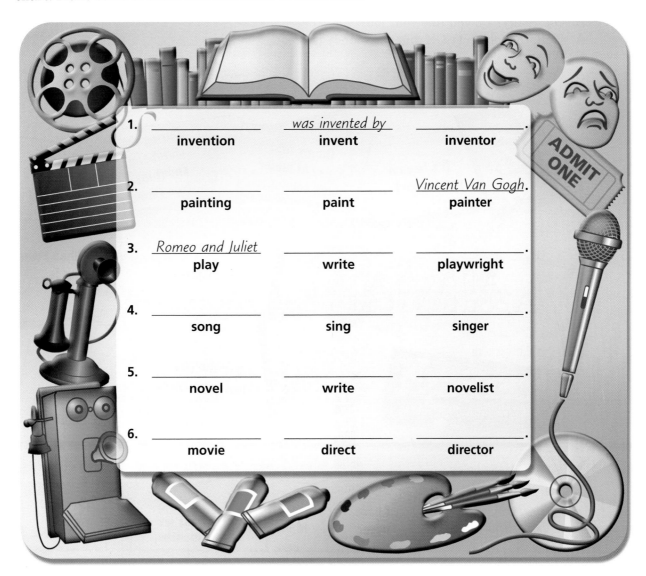

1. _____	*was invented by* _____	_____
invention	invent	inventor
2. _____	_____	*Vincent Van Gogh*.
painting	paint	painter
3. *Romeo and Juliet*	_____	_____
play	write	playwright
4. _____	_____	_____
song	sing	singer
5. _____	_____	_____
novel	write	novelist
6. _____	_____	_____
movie	direct	director

D *Group work* Make a statement about each item to your group members. Ask them to decide which statements are true and which are false.

A: The telephone was invented by Alexander Graham Bell.
B: I think that's false.
C: Really? I'm pretty sure it's true.

LIFE IS LIKE A GAME!

A *Group work* Play the board game. Follow these instructions.

1. Use small pieces of paper with your initials on them as markers.

2. Take turns by tossing a coin:
   If the coin lands face up, move two spaces.
   If the coin lands face down, move one space.

3. Complete the sentence in the space you land on. Others ask two
   follow-up questions to get more information.

A: It's been a year since I started working.
B: Oh, really? Do you like your job?
A: Well, the job's just OK, but the money is great!
C: What do you do?
A: I'm a . . .

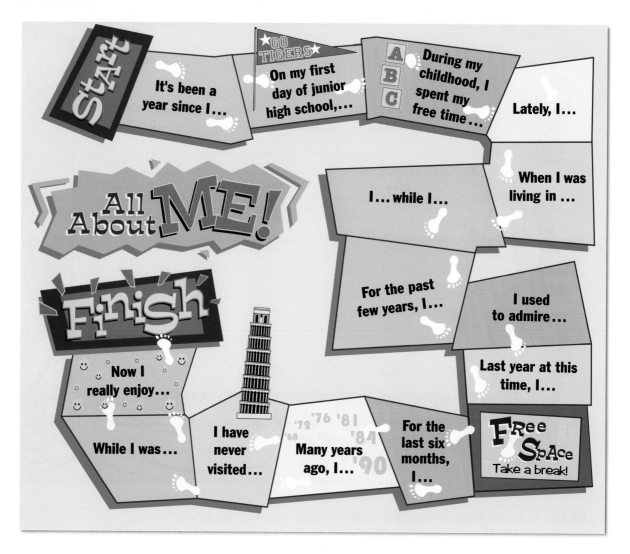

B *Class activity* Tell the class an interesting fact that you learned
about someone in your group.

"Last year at this time, Daniel was hiking in the Swiss Alps!"

A Complete this questionnaire.

What is the name of a TV or movie star . . . ?	
1. that reminds you of someone in your family	....
2. that has beautiful eyes	....
3. who does things to help society	....
4. who has a beautiful speaking voice	....
5. who isn't good-looking but who is very talented	....
What is the name of a TV show or movie . . . ?	
6. that made you feel sad	....
7. that made you laugh a lot	....
8. which scared you	....
9. which had great music	....
10. that was about a ridiculous story	....

B *Pair work* Compare your questionnaires. Ask follow-up questions of your own.

A: What is the name of a TV or movie star that reminds you of someone in your family?
B: Tom Cruise.
A: Who does he remind you of?
B: My brother, Todd.
A: Really? Why?
B: Because he looks like my brother. They have the same smile.

A *Pair work* Look at this scene of a crowded restaurant. What do you think is happening in each of the five situations? Look at people's body language for clues.

A: Why do you think the woman in situation 1 looks upset?
B: Well, she might be having a fight with . . .

A: What do you think the man's gesture in situation 2 means?
B: Maybe it means he . . .

B *Group work* Compare your interpretations. Do you agree or disagree?

Student A

A *Pair work* You and your partner want to get together. You also want to keep time open for other friends, so make up excuses for many of the days. Ask and answer questions to find a day when you are both free. Write your partner's excuses on the calendar.

A: Do you want to go out on the second?
B: I'm sorry. I'm going to my friend's wedding. Are you free on the first?
A: Well, I . . .

JULY

Sunday	Monday	Tuesday	Wednesday	Thursday	Friday	Saturday
					1 dinner with Lynn	**2**
3	**4** class	**5**	**6** ←——————————→ You want to keep these dates free. Make up excuses!	**7**	**8** movie with Tom	**9**
10	**11** ←——————→ You hope a friend calls. Make up excuses!	**12**	**13** jazz club with Mike	**14** theater with Jane	**15**	**16**
17 dinner with office friends	**18** class	**19**	**20** study for exam tomorrow	**21** ←——————————→ You know your old friend will probably be in town. Make up excuses!	**22**	**23**
24 / **31**	**25**	**26** ←——————→ You want to keep these dates free. Make up excuses!	**27**	**28** dinner for Dad's birthday	**29** go dancing with Ted & Sarah	**30** You might have a date with an old school friend. Make up an excuse.

B *Pair work* Now work with another Student A. Discuss the excuses Student B gave you. Decide which excuses were probably true and which ones were probably not true.

A: Anna said that on the ninth she had to stay home and reorganize her clothes closet. That was probably not true.
B: I agree. I think . . .

A What would you do in each of these situations? Circle **a**, **b**, or **c**. If you think you would do something else, write your suggestion next to **d**.

"What Would You Do?"

1. **If an artist friend gave me a large original painting that was ugly, I would . . . .**
   a. say something nice and put it in a closet later
   b. say that I didn't like it
   c. say thank you and hang it on the wall
   d. ....

2. **If I saw a parent spanking a child for no reason, I would . . . .**
   a. do nothing
   b. yell at the parent
   c. call the police
   d. ....

3. **If I saw a student cheating on an exam, I would . . . .**
   a. do nothing
   b. tell the teacher
   c. talk to the student about it after the exam
   d. ....

4. **If I saw my friend's boyfriend or girlfriend with someone other than my friend, I would . . . .**
   a. do nothing
   b. talk to my friend
   c. talk to my friend's boyfriend or girlfriend
   d. ....

5. **If I saw someone standing on a highway next to a car with a flat tire, I would . . . .**
   a. do nothing
   b. stop and help
   c. find the nearest telephone and call the police
   d. ....

B *Group work* Compare your choices for each situation in part A.

A: What would you do if an artist friend gave you an ugly painting?
B: Well, I would probably say that I didn't like it.
C: Really? I would . . .

C *Class activity* Take a class survey. Find out which choice was most popular for each situation. Talk about any other suggestions people added for **d**.

Student B

A *Pair work* You and your partner want to get together. You also want to keep time open for other friends, so make up excuses for many of the days. Ask and answer questions to find a day when you are both free. Write your partner's excuses on the calendar.

A: Do you want to go out on the second?
B: I'm sorry. I'm going to my friend's wedding. Are you free on the first?
A: Well, I . . .

July

Sunday	Monday	Tuesday	Wednesday	Thursday	Friday	Saturday
					1	**2** Sue's wedding
3	**4**	**5** movie with Bob	**6**	**7**	**8**	**9**
	⟵ You want to keep these dates free. Make up excuses! ⟶			⟵ You don't want to make plans in case you want to get away for a few days. Make up excuses! ⟶		
10 visit Mom and Dad	**11** office party	**12**	**13** photography workshop at school	**14**	**15**	**16**
					⟵ Maybe an old friend will call. Make up excuses! ⟶	
17 visit Grandma	**18**	**19** museum with Craig	**20**	**21**	**22** party at Amy's	**23** baseball game with Jim
24 family get-together **31**	**25** You need a break. Make up an excuse!	**26** book group meeting	**27**	**28** need to work late tonight	**29**	**30**

B *Pair work* Now work with another Student B. Discuss the excuses Student A gave you. Decide which excuses were probably true and which ones were probably not true.

A: Joe said that on the sixth he had to stay home and reorganize his clothes closet. That was probably not true.
B: I agree. I think . . .

Units 1–16 Self-study

1 CHILDHOOD SUMMERS

A ▶ Listen to Kim and Jeff talk about their childhood summers. What three things do they have in common?

....

B ▶ Listen again. What were their summers like? Complete the chart.

	Their pets	Their favorite places	Their hobbies
1. Kim	....	....	....
	....	....	....
2. Jeff	....	....	....
	....	....	....

2 TOURIST INFORMATION

A ▶ Listen to some tourists ask for information at their hotel. Write what each person needs to do.

Needs	Responses
1. *exchange some money*	☐ a. There's one right across the street from here. ☒ b. It's past 10:00. They should be open now.
2.	☒ a. It stays open until 6 P.M. ☐ b. It opens at 9 A.M.
3.	☐ a. Only once a day. We really need more trains! ☒ b. You can follow this street all the way there.
4.	☒ a. It's eight blocks away. There aren't enough taxi stands in this area. ☐ b. Walk down to Grand Street. You can catch the subway there.
5.	☒ a. It costs twenty dollars a day. ☐ b. You can buy a special pass to go anywhere in the city.
6.	☒ a. Try the café on the corner. I think it's open until midnight. ☐ b. We need more vegetarian restaurants. The only one is on Ninth Avenue.

B ▶ Listen again. Check (✓) the correct response.

3 APARTMENT FOR RENT

A ▶ Listen to two people call about apartment advertisements.
Do you think the woman is going to rent the apartment? ☐ Yes ☐ No
Do you think the man is going to rent the apartment? ☐ Yes ☐ No

B ▶ Listen again. Which adjectives best describe each apartment?
Write **1** for the first apartment or **2** for the second apartment.

.... bright   .... dark   .... noisy   .... quiet   .... safe
.... dangerous   .... expensive   .... old   .... reasonable   .... spacious

4 HAVE YOU TRIED IT?

A ▶ Listen to two people shop for food. What foods have they tried?
Write **H** for Heidi or **P** for Peter.

H ceviche   H red chili peppers   H Thai fried noodles   P coconut curry

B ▶ Listen again. How do you make ceviche? Number the pictures
from 1 to 5.

5 VACATION PLANS

A ▶ Listen to Cynthia discuss her vacation plans with Paul.
Check (✓) the things she talks about doing.

☐ fishing   ☒ going abroad   ☒ seeing another city
☑ camping   ☒ staying home   ☐ taking cooking lessons
☐ shopping   ☒ going to the beach ☐ going to the mountains

B ▶ Listen again. For each activity you checked, write Paul's advice.

1. Pack a first-aid and because   4. Make a reservation
2. Passport - visa   5. Do something fun
3. Don't go to beach

6 SIMPLE REQUESTS

A ▶ Listen to people make requests. Check (✓) the thing each person talks about.

1. ☐ the radio   ☐ the window   ☐ the dog
2. ☐ the coat   ☐ the shoes   ☐ the magazine
3. ☐ the baby   ☐ the grandfather   ☐ the dog
4. ☐ the yard   ☐ the TV   ☐ the window
5. ☐ the TV   ☐ the coat   ☐ the lamp
6. ☐ the toys   ☐ the books   ☐ the dishes

B ▶ Listen again. Write the words that helped you choose each answer.

1. ....   3. ....   5. ....
2. ....   4. ....   6. ....

7 COMPUTER SUPPORT

A ▶ Listen to Janet call a computer support center for help.
What is Janet's problem?

☐ She used the wrong keyboard.   ☐ She downloaded a virus.
☐ She didn't know the screen saver was on.

B ▶ Listen again. Check (✓) the correct answer(s).

1. What does Janet use her laptop for?

☐ writing short stories   ☐ writing e-mails   ☐ playing DVDs
☐ surfing the Internet   ☐ playing games   ☐ downloading music

2. How can Janet protect her monitor?

☐ close her laptop   ☐ turn on the screen saver   ☐ leave her computer on all day

8 TRICK OR TREAT!

A ▶ Listen to someone talk about Halloween. Check (✓) True or False for each statement.

	True	False
1. October 31 is the day when people wear costumes.	☐	☐
2. During the 400s, people dressed up on October 31 to scare away the dead.	☐	☐
3. People believed that Halloween marked the end of spring.	☐	☐
4. In the U.S., Halloween is the time when adults "trick or treat."	☐	☐
5. On Halloween, children go to their neighbors' houses to ask for money.	☐	☐
6. These days, Halloween is a night when adults go to parties or parades.	☐	☐

B ▶ Listen again. For the statements you marked false, write the correct information.

 **TOO MUCH TECHNOLOGY?**

A ▶ Listen to Jimmy and his grandfather talk about technology. Check (✓) the things his grandfather has used.

☐ an album

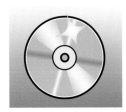
☐ a CD

☐ the Internet

☐ an MP3 player

☐ a cassette

☐ a cell phone

☐ a laptop

☐ a radio

B ▶ Listen again and answer these questions.

1. What does Jimmy think might happen to technology in the future?
2. What is one advantage of future technology?
3. What is one disadvantage of future technology?

10 ELECTION DEBATE

A ▶ Listen to an election debate. Write **A** for André or **J** for Jeri beside the adjective that best describes each person.

.... creative .... hardworking .... moody
.... critical .... impatient .... organized
.... efficient .... level-headed .... reliable

B ▶ Listen again and complete the chart.

	André			Jeri		
How good is each candidate at . . . ?	good	OK	so-so	good	OK	so-so
1. working with people	☐	☐	☐	☐	☐	☐
2. solving problems	☐	☐	☐	☐	☐	☐
How does each candidate like . . . ?	likes	doesn't mind	hates	likes	doesn't mind	hates
3. helping people	☐	☐	☐	☐	☐	☐
4. making mistakes	☐	☐	☐	☐	☐	☐

11 THE STATUE OF LIBERTY

A ▶ Listen to two tourists on a boat tour of New York Harbor.
Why doesn't the man want to go inside the Statue of Liberty?

☐ It's closed to visitors. ☐ There's no elevator. ☐ There isn't enough time.

B ▶ Listen again. Correct the seven mistakes in the text.

> *France*
> The Statue of Liberty is located in New York Harbor. The people of ~~Canada~~ gave the statue to the United States. The statue was designed by a French sculptor. Hundreds of people from all over the world visit the Statue of Liberty every year. There are 54 steps to the top of the crown. The statue was manufactured in the United States and shipped to New York. In 1986, it was assembled on Liberty Island, which took nine months. Visitors may climb the stairs to the top of the statue.

12 WHAT A LUCKY BREAK!

A ▶ Listen to Stacy and Richard talk about their careers.
Who had a lucky break? ☐ Stacy ☐ Richard

B ▶ Listen again. Number the events for each person from 1 to 5.

Stacy	Richard
.... She moved to Los Angeles.	.... He sent his novel to publishers.
.... She was offered a position on a new show.	.... He tried to make a living as a writer.
.... She got a job as an assistant at a TV station.	.... He got a job at a hardware store.
.... She graduated from drama school.	.... He majored in English literature in college.
.... The regular announcer got sick.	.... His work was rejected eight times.

13 THIS BOOK LOOKS INTERESTING.

A ▶ Listen to people talk about a book. Match each character with two descriptions.

.... 1. the owner   .... 3. the jockey
.... 2. the trainer   .... 4. the horse

a. half blind	c. millionaire	e. small	g. outspoken
b. cowboy	d. odd-looking	f. quiet	h. well-educated

B ▶ Listen again. Complete these sentences with relative clauses from the conversation.

1. The owner was a man . . .   3. The jockey was a man . . .
2. The trainer was a man . . .   4. Seabiscuit was a horse . . .

14 POLICE PATROL

A ▶ Listen to four conversations. Number the pictures from 1 to 4.

[ ] BUCKLE UP ITS THE LAW   [ ] (no cars sign)   [ ] (dog on leash sign)   [ ] (no parking sign)

....

B ▶ Listen again. Write each rule under the correct picture.

1. You can't park here.
2. You've got to put your dog on a leash.
3. Cars aren't allowed on this street.
4. You have to fasten your seat belt.

15 UNFORTUNATE SITUATIONS

A ▶ Listen to people describe situations. Check (✓) the correct response.

1. [ ] He should have locked the car.
   [ ] He shouldn't have left money in the car.

3. [ ] He should have written it down.
   [ ] He shouldn't have remembered the dinner.

....

2. [ ] She should have spent the money.
   [ ] She shouldn't have gone shopping.

4. [ ] She should have borrowed a friend's car.
   [ ] She shouldn't have lent her car to a friend.

....

B ▶ Listen again. Write your own response for each situation.

16 DON'T TELL ANYONE . . .

A ▶ Listen to a telephone conversation. What excuse did Susan give Bill?

[ ] She had dinner plans.   [ ] She was going to the movies.   [ ] She wasn't feeling well.

B ▶ Listen again. Read the voice mail Grace left another friend. Then correct the six errors in her message.

Hi, it's Grace. I just talked to Bill, and you won't believe what happened! Bill said that Jack saw Susan and her father having lunch together last week. Bill and Susan were supposed to go shopping together, but Susan called the day before to say she couldn't make it. Well, Bill said he understood, and told her to stay home and get something to eat. But instead of staying home, she went out! Oh, by the way, don't say anything, OK? I promised Bill I wouldn't tell anyone.

Self-study audio scripts

1 Childhood summers

A Listen to Kim and Jeff talk about their childhood summers. What three things do they have in common?

JEFF: Hey, Kim, are these pictures of you when you were a kid?

KIM: Yeah. That's me with my dog. We used to spend a week at my uncle's beach house every summer.

JEFF: Hmm. When I was a kid, we used to take our dog and cat with us to the beach every year. Summers were always so much fun!

KIM: Yeah. I used to spend all day playing up in our tree house. I even brought my pet rabbit up there!

JEFF: Really? Our neighbors down the street had a great tree house. My brother and I used to sneak up there to play chess and read comic books.

KIM: Really? I remember that some kids used to leave their comic books in our tree house, but we never saw the kids.

JEFF: That's funny. What else did you use to do up there?

KIM: We used to climb up and make scrapbooks out of pictures we cut out of magazines. We also painted animals on the walls.

JEFF: Huh? What kinds of animals?

KIM: Dogs, horses, my rabbit…

JEFF: Wait a minute. Was your uncle's house on Glenn Avenue?

KIM: That was *you*?!

B Listen again. What were their summers like? Complete the chart.

2 Tourist information

A Listen to some tourists ask for information at their hotel. Write what each person needs to do.

1. MAN: Do you know when the banks open? I have to exchange some money.

2. WOMAN: Could you tell me what time the post office closes? I need to mail some postcards.

3. MAN: I'd like to buy some souvenirs. Can you tell me how to get to the outdoor market?

4. WOMAN: I need to go to the airport. Can you tell me where the nearest taxi stand is?

5. MAN: Do you know how much it costs to use the parking garage? I need to park my car.

6. WOMAN: I'd like to get something to eat. Could you tell me which restaurants serve dinner this late?

B Listen again. Check the correct response.

3 Apartment for rent

A Listen to two people call about apartment advertisements. Do you think the woman is going to rent the apartment? Do you think the man is going to rent the apartment?

MAN 1: [*phone rings*] Creative Rentals. Good morning.

WOMAN 1: Hello. I'm calling about the apartment you have for rent.

MAN 1: Yes. What can I tell you about it?

WOMAN 1: Where is it, exactly?

MAN 1: It's on King Street, just off the freeway.

WOMAN 1: Oh, near the freeway. Can you hear the traffic?

MAN 1: Yes, I'm afraid you do hear some. But the apartment has lots of space. It has three bedrooms and a very large living room.

WOMAN 1: I see. And is it in a new building?

MAN 1: Well, the building is over 50 years old.

WOMAN 1: Uh-huh. Well, I'll think about it. I wish it weren't so close to the freeway.

MAN 1: Well, if you want to see it, just give me a call.

WOMAN 1: OK, thank you.

MAN 1: Thanks for calling. Bye.

WOMAN 2: [*phone rings*] Town and City Rentals. How can I help you?

MAN 2: Hi. Umm . . . is that apartment you advertised still available?

WOMAN 2: Yes, it is.

MAN 2: Oh, good. Umm . . . listen. I, I can't pay too much, so the low price is really good for me.

WOMAN 2: Great.

MAN 2: Is it a big place?

WOMAN 2: No. It's two rooms, plus the kitchen and bathroom.

MAN 2: And is it a safe area to live?

WOMAN 2: Well, I can tell you I've lived in this neighborhood for five years and I've never heard about anybody having a problem.

MAN 2: Oh, that's good. Uh . . . let's see. Oh, yeah. Does the apartment have a lot of windows?

WOMAN 2: Windows? Yes, there are plenty of windows. But unfortunately, there's another building right next door. I wish the apartment were brighter, but there isn't much light, really.

MAN 2: Oh. Well, I'm never around during the day, anyway. Is it all right if I come look at it?

WOMAN 2: Sure. Just tell me when you want to see it.

B Listen again. Which adjectives best describe each apartment? Write **1** for the first apartment or **2** for the second apartment.

4 Have you tried it?

A Listen to two people shop for food. What foods have they tried? Write **H** for Heidi or **P** for Peter.

HEIDI: Over here, Peter! The fish looks so fresh. We could make ceviche this weekend. I love ceviche! Have you tried it?

PETER: No, I haven't. How do you make it?

HEIDI: Well, first you cut up the seafood in bite-size pieces.

PETER: So we'll need different kinds of fish?

HEIDI: Yeah. Let's get three kinds.

PETER: OK. Then what?

HEIDI: Then you mix the seafood with chili peppers.

PETER: Here are some red chili peppers, but I don't know what they're like. Have you tried this kind?

HEIDI: Yes, I tried them once. They were very spicy!

PETER: Good. I love spicy food. What next?

HEIDI: Next, you add lime juice and mix it in. After that, you put the seafood in the refrigerator to marinate.

PETER: You don't cook it?

HEIDI: No, you just marinate it overnight. Finally, you put the mixture on some lettuce and serve it!

PETER: OK, so what are we having tonight?

HEIDI: Oh! I know how to make a great dish – it's Thai fried noodles with chicken.

PETER: That sounds interesting. I'd like to try it, but I ate chicken for lunch. I really love coconut curry. Have you ever had it?

HEIDI: No, but it sounds good. Let's make that!

PETER: OK. Um, there are some spices right over there. Let's get some and then go. I'm getting hungry!

B Listen again. How do you make ceviche? Number the pictures from 1 to 5.

5 Vacation plans

A Listen to Cynthia discuss her vacation plans with Paul. Check the things she talks about doing.

PAUL: So, Cynthia, what are you doing with your time off?

CYNTHIA: I don't know. I haven't decided yet. I might go camping somewhere and just enjoy nature for a couple of weeks.

PAUL: Well, you'd better pack a first-aid kit and be careful. It could be dangerous!

CYNTHIA: Uh, yeah. Or maybe I'll go abroad and study a foreign language.

PAUL: Hmm. But there probably isn't enough time. You'll have to get a passport and maybe even a visa.

CYNTHIA: OK, so maybe I'll go to the beach and catch up on some reading.

PAUL: You shouldn't go to the beach at this time of year. It'll be too crowded!

CYNTHIA: Well, then I might go to another city and visit some museums and art galleries.

PAUL: You need to make a reservation right away! The plane ticket is going to be so expensive now!

CYNTHIA: Well, then I probably won't go anywhere. I'll just stay home and watch TV!

PAUL: That sounds boring. Why don't you do something more fun?

B Listen again. For each activity you checked, write Paul's advice.

6 Simple requests

A Listen to people make requests. Check the thing each person talks about.

1. MAN: Would you mind turning it down, please? I'm trying to read and I can't concentrate with it on so loud.

2. WOMAN: Can you pick them up? You need to put them away as soon as you take them off instead of just leaving them on the floor for someone to trip over.

3. MAN: Could you take him out for a walk? He hasn't been out for a couple of hours. Don't forget to keep him on the leash.

4. WOMAN: Would you please close it? When you leave it open, the wind blows and makes the room really cold.

5. MAN: Can you turn that on for me? It's getting dark in here, and I can't see what I'm reading.

6. WOMAN: Would you mind not leaving them on the counter when they're dirty? At least put them in the sink.

B Listen again. Write the words that helped you choose each answer.

7 Computer support

A Listen to Janet call a computer support center for help. What is Janet's problem?

MATT: [*phone rings*] Support center, this is Matt.

JANET: Uh, hi, Matt. I'm having problems with my laptop.

MATT: What's the problem?

JANET: I'm not really sure.

MATT: Well, what do you see when you turn your laptop on?

JANET: It comes on at first, but then it goes black after a while. I think the monitor may be broken. Or maybe I have a virus.

MATT: Hmm. What do you normally use your laptop for?

JANET: I use it for writing e-mails and surfing the Internet. I also use it to play computer games.

MATT: And how long do you usually leave it on?

JANET: Well, I also download music sometimes, so I leave it on all day while I'm doing other things.

MATT: Uh-huh. Always remember to turn on the screen saver when you're away from your laptop. Your monitor will last longer that way.

JANET: What's a screen saver?

MATT: It's something that comes on while you're not using your monitor, to protect it. Be sure to turn it on.

JANET: OK. And what does it look like when it comes on?

MATT: Well, it's black unless you download something else to use.

JANET: It's black? Oh, and what happens when you use the keyboard?

MATT: Your monitor comes back on when you use the keyboard. You can also move the mouse to "wake up" the monitor.

JANET: Uh, OK, well . . . I don't think I have a problem with my monitor anymore . . . it was just the, uh, screen saver.

MATT: Well, don't forget to download a new screen saver. Then next time your monitor goes black, you'll know it's really broken!

B Listen again. Check the correct answer(s).

8 Trick or treat!

A Listen to someone talk about Halloween. Check True or False for each statement.

MAN: One fall day, as you walk down the street, you might see ghosts, strange animals, and other weird things. What's going on? It's probably October 31st, or Halloween. Halloween is a day when people go out wearing costumes and colorful makeup.

Some people think that Halloween started in Ireland during the 400s. October 31st was the end of summer, and people believed that everyone who died during the year came back on that day. To scare away the dead, people put on costumes and went out into the streets to make noise.

Different cultures have different ways of celebrating Halloween. In the United States, it's the night when children dress up in costumes and go to neighbors' houses to "trick or treat," or ask for candy. Some adults wear funny or scary costumes and go to parties or parades. Halloween has become a fun holiday for both adults and children.

B Listen again. For the statements you marked false, write the correct information.

Self-study audio scripts

9 Too much technology?

A Listen to Jimmy and his grandfather talk about technology. Check the things his grandfather has used.

GRANDFATHER: What are you listening to, Jimmy? Is that a radio?

JIMMY: No, it's an MP3 player.

GRANDFATHER: An MP3 player? What's that?

JIMMY: It's a machine that plays music that I download from my computer.

GRANDFATHER: Hmm. When I was a child, we listened to the radio. Then, people listened to albums, and later, to cassettes. Everything changes so fast these days!

JIMMY: Yeah. Now, most people get music from CDs or the Internet. In five years, I bet there will be other ways.

GRANDFATHER: CDs, huh? Well, I guess if I don't pay attention, I'll miss out on a lot of new technology.

JIMMY: Right. Like just a few years ago, they made a cell phone that also surfs the Internet. Soon, we might not even need laptops or MP3 players – everything will be in one piece of technology.

GRANDFATHER: Do you really think so?

JIMMY: Yeah, and if all the technology is in one piece of equipment, you'll have fewer things to carry.

GRANDFATHER: Exactly! And if you don't need a laptop, an MP3 player, and a cell phone, you won't need such a big allowance, right?

JIMMY: Uh, well . . .

B Listen again and answer these questions.

10 Election debate

A Listen to an election debate. Write **A** for André or **J** for Jeri beside the adjective that best describes each person.

TEACHER: Welcome to our debate! The candidates for class president this year are André and Jeri. Please introduce yourselves and tell us why you'd be a good president.

ANDRÉ: Hi, I'm André. I think I'd be a great class president because I'm reliable, and I'm very creative.

JERI: Hi, everyone. I'm Jeri and I'm really good at organizing. I'm also efficient, and I'm hardworking.

TEACHER: How good are you at working with people? André?

ANDRÉ: I'm really good at working with people. And I'd make a good president because I am always level-headed. Most people think I'm easy to talk to.

TEACHER: And Jeri?

JERI: I'm OK at working with people. Sometimes I'm a little impatient, but I'm never critical.

TEACHER: OK! Next question. André, can you solve problems easily?

ANDRÉ: Well, it takes a lot of work to solve problems for a whole class, but I think I'm good at it. I really like helping people, and like I said, I'm very creative. Sometimes a problem just needs a creative solution!

TEACHER: OK, Jeri, what about you?

JERI: I like helping people, too. I'm so-so at solving problems, but if the solution doesn't work, I always ask someone for help. I can't stand making mistakes.

ANDRÉ: Oh, I don't mind. If you don't make mistakes, you won't learn anything!

TEACHER: That's a good point, André. Well, we're out of time. Thanks to our candidates for participating, and don't forget to vote on Thursday! [*applause*]

B Listen again and complete the chart.

11 The Statue of Liberty

A Listen to two tourists on a boat tour of New York Harbor. Why doesn't the man want to go inside the Statue of Liberty?

GUIDE: We are now approaching the famous Statue of Liberty, which has welcomed visitors to New York Harbor since 1886.

MAN: Wow! Look at it.

WOMAN: Incredible, isn't it?

GUIDE: The statue was given to the United States by the people of France. It was designed by the French sculptor Bartholdi.

MAN: It's really huge. Do we get to go inside?

WOMAN: I think I can climb the stairs all the way up to the crown.

MAN: Stairs? There's no elevator?

WOMAN: Well . . .

GUIDE: The Statue of Liberty is a major tourist attraction, and every year it is visited by millions of people from all over the world. There are 354 steps to the top of the crown.

MAN: Did you hear that? 354 steps!

WOMAN: Oh, come on, you can do it! People do it every day!

MAN: But . . .

GUIDE: The statue was manufactured in France, and shipped to New York in 1884. It arrived a year later. Then it was assembled on Liberty Island, where it stands today. Putting it together took four months.

MAN: I'm not feeling so good. . . .

WOMAN: Oh, stop! It'll be fun!

GUIDE: Please be back at the boat in 30 minutes. Unfortunately, the statue is currently closed to visitors. You may walk around the island, but you may not climb the stairs to the top.

MAN: Hey, let's go! What are you waiting for?

B Listen again. Correct the seven mistakes in the text.

12 What a lucky break!

A Listen to Stacy and Richard talk about their careers. Who had a lucky break?

RICHARD: How did you get into TV announcing, Stacy?

STACY: Well, when I graduated from drama school, I moved to Los Angeles to look for work as an actress. I was going to auditions every day, but I never got any parts. And I was running out of money.

RICHARD: So, what did you do?

STACY: I got a job as an assistant at a TV station. While I was working there, the regular announcer got sick and they asked me to fill in. I guess I did a good job, because within a few weeks, they offered me a position on a new show!

RICHARD: Wow, what a lucky break!

STACY: So, Richard, what did you do after you graduated?

RICHARD: Well, I majored in English literature in college.

STACY: Uh-huh.

RICHARD: So when I graduated, I tried to make my living as a writer.

STACY: Oh, really?

RICHARD: Yeah. See, I've written a novel and I've sent it to eight publishers, but they all, uh, rejected it. Say, would you like to read it? I have it right here with me.

STACY: Well, I'd love to read it, Richard, . . . but not right now. Uh, so do you have a job or anything?

RICHARD: Oh, yes. I'm in sales.

STACY: Oh? Where?

RICHARD: Actually, I've been working for the last month as a salesclerk in a hardware store. But when my novel sells, I know I'll be a best-selling author and I'll make lots of money.

B Listen again. Number the events for each person from 1 to 5.

13 This book looks interesting.

A Listen to people talk about a book. Match each character with two descriptions.

WOMAN: This book looks interesting.

MAN: Oh, I read that! It's fascinating. It's about a horse named Seabiscuit that won a big race.

WOMAN: What's so great about a horse winning a race?

MAN: Well, it happened at a time when the country was struggling with the Great Depression, and people became very excited by the story of this horse.

WOMAN: Why is that?

MAN: Well, it involved an unusual cast of characters. The horse's owner was a millionaire who was very loud and outspoken. And the trainer was a quiet man who used to be a cowboy in the American West.

WOMAN: Those two sound pretty different.

MAN: It gets better. The jockey was a well-educated fighter who was also half blind. And then Seabiscuit was a little odd-looking – he was considered too small to be a racehorse.

WOMAN: Hmm. They do sound unusual.

MAN: That's the point. All these strange characters came together to make Seabiscuit into a champion. The whole country was amazed.

WOMAN: Hmm. Maybe I'll read it.

MAN: Well, the movie is really good, too.

WOMAN: Oh, there's a movie?

MAN: Yeah, it's the one that stars Tobey Maguire.

WOMAN: Oh, I've heard about it! It's supposed to be fantastic!

MAN: Well, then, why don't we rent the DVD?

WOMAN: You don't mind seeing it again?

MAN: Not at all. You rent the DVD, and I'll make some popcorn.

B Listen again. Complete these sentences with relative clauses from the conversation.

14 Police patrol

A Listen to four conversations. Number the pictures from 1 to 4.

1. WOMAN 1: What's the problem, officer?

OFFICER: Well, you can't park here.

WOMAN 1: Oh. I didn't see a sign.

OFFICER: There's a sign right there, behind the tree.

2. MAN 1: What is that police officer trying to tell us?

WOMAN 2: Uh, it probably means he wants us to go over there.

MAN 1: But we didn't do anything wrong.

WOMAN 2: Oh, look, there's a sign. We've got to put Fluffy on a leash.

3. MAN 2: Excuse me, officer, can we drive through here?

OFFICER: No, cars aren't allowed on this street. It's for pedestrians only.

MAN 2: How can I get to the library from here?

OFFICER: Go two more blocks to First Avenue. You can drive on that street.

4. WOMAN 2: Why is that traffic officer waving at us?

MAN 1: I don't know. It must mean he wants us to stop.

WOMAN 2: No, he's making a diagonal motion with his hand. He looks annoyed.

MAN 1: Ohhh, it probably means we have to fasten our seat belts! I'm wearing mine . . . are you?

WOMAN 2: Well, uh . . . no.

B Listen again. Write each rule under the correct picture.

15 Unfortunate situations

A Listen to people describe situations. Check the correct response.

1. MAN 1: I parked my car downtown and left my briefcase on the back seat. It had some money in it. I locked the car, of course, but when I came back, someone had broken the window and taken my briefcase.

2. WOMAN 1: I found a hundred-dollar bill in my neighbor's driveway. My neighbor was away, so the money probably wasn't his. Anyway, I took the money and went shopping. I bought a cool new jacket and a fabulous skirt. Now I feel bad.

3. MAN 2: My aunt invited me over for dinner. Unfortunately, I forgot to write it down. The day I was supposed to go to her house, a friend invited me to see a movie with him, and I completely forgot about dinner.

4. WOMAN 2: I lent my car to a friend who doesn't have a driver's license. While he was driving, he had an accident and caused more than five hundred dollars' worth of damage to my car.

B Listen again. Write your own response for each situation.

16 Don't tell anyone . . .

A Listen to a telephone conversation. What excuse did Susan give Bill?

GRACE: [*phone rings*] Hello?

BILL: Grace, it's Bill.

GRACE: What's up?

BILL: I'm so annoyed! Jack told me he saw Susan and her ex-boyfriend having dinner together!

GRACE: Really? When?

BILL: Last night. Susan and I were supposed to go to the movies. Then she called at the last minute and said she wasn't feeling well.

GRACE: Oh, so she told you she couldn't go.

BILL: Yeah. I said I understood. I told her that she should stay home and get some rest.

GRACE: Good, so you expressed your concern.

BILL: Yeah, but instead of staying home, she went out!

GRACE: That's terrible! She shouldn't have done that.

BILL: I know. She shouldn't have made an excuse. She should've just told me the truth! Listen, don't tell anyone, OK?

GRACE: Right. Uh, I have to go. I'll talk to you later.

B Listen again. Read the voice mail Grace left another friend. Then correct the six errors in her message.

Self-study audio scripts

Self-study answer key

1
A both had a dog; both used to go to the beach every summer; both used to play in a tree house

B

	pets	*places*	*hobbies*
1. Kim	dog	beach	make scrapbooks
	rabbit	tree house	paint
2. Jeff	dog	beach	play chess
	cat	tree house	read comic books

2
A 1. exchange some money   4. go to the airport
2. mail some postcards   5. park his car
3. buy some souvenirs   6. get something to eat

B 1. b; 2. a; 3. b; 4. a; 5. a; 6. a

3
A No; Yes

B 1: noisy; old; spacious
2: dark; reasonable; safe

4
A H: ceviche; red chili peppers; Thai fried noodles
P: coconut curry

B 2, 4, 5, 1, 3

5
A camping, going abroad, going to the beach, seeing another city, staying home

B 1. You'd better pack a first-aid kit and be careful.
2. You have to get a passport and a visa.
3. You shouldn't go to the beach.
4. You need to make a reservation.
5. Why don't you do something fun?

6
A/B 1. the radio (loud)
2. the shoes (them)
3. the dog (him, walk, leash)
4. the window (close, open, wind, cold)
5. the lamp (dark, reading)
6. the dishes (them, counter, dirty, sink)

7
A She didn't know the screen saver was on.

B 1. surfing the Internet; writing e-mails; playing games; downloading music
2. turn on the screen saver

8
A/B 1. True   4. False (*children* "trick or treat")
2. True   5. False (ask for *candy*)
3. False (end   6. True
of *summer*)

9
A a radio; an album; a cassette

B 1. Everything will be in one piece of technology.
2. You'll have fewer things to carry.
3. You won't need a big allowance.

10
A A: creative; level-headed; reliable
J: efficient; hardworking; impatient; organized

B

	Andre	*Jeri*
1. working with people	good	OK
2. solving problems	good	so-so
3. helping people	likes	likes
4. making mistakes	doesn't mind	hates

11
A There's no elevator.

B

1. ~~Canada~~	France	5. ~~1986~~	1886
2. ~~Hundreds~~	Millions	6. ~~nine~~	four
3. ~~54~~	354	7. ~~may~~	may not
4. ~~the United States~~	France		

12
A Stacy

B Stacy: 2, 5, 3, 1, 4
Richard: 3, 2, 5, 1, 4

13
A 1. c, g; 2. b, f; 3. a, h; 4. d, e

B (Possible answers)
1. who was outspoken.   3. who was half blind.
2. that used to be a cowboy.   4. that won a big race.

14
A/B 4. You have to fasten your seat belt.
3. Cars aren't allowed on this street.
2. You've got to put your dog on a leash.
1. You can't park here.

15
A 1. He shouldn't have left money in the car.
2. She shouldn't have gone shopping.
3. He should have written it down.
4. She shouldn't have lent her car to a friend.

B Answers will vary.

16
A She wasn't feeling well.

B

1. ~~father~~	ex-boyfriend
2. ~~lunch~~	dinner
3. ~~week~~	night
4. ~~shopping~~	to the movies
5. ~~the day before~~	at the last minute
6. ~~something to eat~~	some rest

Appendix

Countries and nationalities

This is a partial list of countries, many of which are presented in this book.

Argentina	Argentine	France	French
Australia	Australian	Germany	German
Austria	Austrian	Greece	Greek
Brazil	Brazilian	Hungary	Hungarian
Bolivia	Bolivian	India	Indian
Canada	Canadian	Indonesia	Indonesian
Chile	Chilean	Ireland	Irish
China	Chinese	Italy	Italian
Colombia	Colombian	Japan	Japanese
Costa Rica	Costa Rican	Korea	Korean
Czech Republic	Czech	Malaysia	Malaysian
Ecuador	Ecuadorian	Mexico	Mexican
Egypt	Egyptian	Morocco	Moroccan
England	English	New Zealand	New Zealander

Paraguay	Paraguayan
the Philippines	Filipino
Portugal	Portuguese
Russia	Russian
Singapore	Singaporean
Spain	Spanish
Switzerland	Swiss
Thailand	Thai
Turkey	Turkish
Peru	Peruvian
the United Kingdom	British
the United States	American
Uruguay	Uruguayan
Vietnam	Vietnamese

Irregular verbs

Present	Past	Participle	Present	Past	Participle
(be) am/is, are	was, were	been	keep	kept	kept
break	broke	broken	lose	lost	lost
bring	brought	brought	meet	met	met
build	built	built	put	put	put
buy	bought	bought	ride	rode	ridden
come	came	come	ring	rang	rung
do	did	done	run	ran	run
drink	drank	drunk	see	saw	seen
drive	drove	driven	send	sent	sent
eat	ate	eaten	set	set	set
fall	fell	fallen	speak	spoke	spoken
feel	felt	felt	stand	stood	stood
find	found	found	steal	stole	stolen
fly	flew	flown	swim	swam	swum
forget	forgot	forgotten	take	took	taken
give	gave	given	teach	taught	taught
go	went	gone	tell	told	told
grow	grew	grown	think	thought	thought
have	had	had	wear	wore	worn
hear	heard	heard	write	wrote	written

Comparative and superlative adjectives

Adjectives with -er and -est

big	dingy	large	new	shabby
bright	dirty	long	nice	short
busy	far	loud	noisy	slow
cheap	fast	messy	old	small
clean	heavy	near	quiet	tall
dark	huge	neat	safe	young

Adjectives with more and most

average	crowded	famous	private
beautiful	dangerous	important	serious
boring	delicious	interesting	spacious
comfortable	difficult	modern	special
convenient	exciting	patient	terrible
cramped	expensive	popular	unusual

Irregular adjectives

good → better → best   bad → worse → the worst

Acknowledgments

Illustrations

Jessica Abel IA7
Rob De Bank 64, 75
Tim Foley 43 (*top*)
Travis Foster 20, 39, 40, 48, 90, 97, IA3
Jeff Grunewald 48
Adam Hurwitz 24 (*bottom*), 37, 44
Randy Jones v, 2, 3, 16, 24 (*top*), 30, 31, 36 (*top*), 49, 62, 66, 67, 80, 81, 92 (*top*), 93 (*bottom*), 99, 100, 101, 106, 108, 109, IA1, IA6, IA14, IA15

Mark Kaufman 25
Scott Pollack IA9
Amy Saidens IA10
Dan Vasconcellos 15, 41, 68, 82, 110, 111, 112
Sam Whitehead 5, 6, 19, 33, 38, 43 (*bottom*), 47, 53, 54, 92 (*bottom*), 93 (*top*), IA4, IA13
Jeff Wong 9, 11, 22, 36 (*bottom*), 46, 58, 60, 79, 94, 102, 104, 107

Photo credits

2 (*left*) © Robert Daly/Getty Images; (*right*) © Peter Nicholson/Getty Images
5 © Ed Bock/Corbis
6 © Getty Images
7 © Reuters/Corbis
8 (*top row, left to right*) © Corbis; © Bob Rowan/Progressive Image/Corbis; (*bottom row, left to right*) © Paul A. Souders/Corbis; © Paul Harris/Getty Images; © age Fotostock
13 (*left to right*) Courtesy of Outrider; courtesy of PowerSki; courtesy of Trikke Inc.; courtesy of Wheelman Inc.
14 © SuperStock
17 (*left*) © Alamy; (*right*) © Jeremy Cockayne/Arcaid/Alamy
18 (*top*) © Roger Ressmeyer/Corbis; (*bottom*) Claudio Santini/Beateworks/Alamy
21 © Ghislain&Marie David de Lossy/Getty Images
22 (*left to right*) © Taesam Do/Getty Images; © Paulo Friedman/International Stock; © George Kerrigan; © Peter Johansky/Envision
23 © Bill Bachman/PhotoEdit
25 (*top*) © Corbis; (*middle row*) © George Kerrigan
26 (*top row, left to right*) © David Jeffrey/Getty Images; © Joel Glenn/Getty Images; © Ed Bock/Corbis; © Roy Morsch/Corbis; (*bottom*) © George Kerrigan
27 (*top*) © Alamy; (*bottom*) © Zefa/Masterfile
29 (*top*) © George Kerrigan; (*bottom*) © Shizuo Kimbayashi/AP/Wide World Photos
30 (*left to right*) © Ghislain&Marie David de Lossy/Getty Images; © Owen Franken/Corbis; © Joyce Choo/Corbis; © George Shelley/Corbis
34 (*top*) © Gavin Hellier/Jon Arnold Images/Alamy; (*bottom*) © age Fotostock
35 © Brad Wrobleski/Masterfile
38 © Getty Images
42 © Corbis
45 (*top*) © Pitchal Frederic/Corbis/Sygma; (*bottom*) © Roger Tulley/Getty Images
47 (*top to bottom*) © Michael Keller/Index Stock; © Jody Dole/Getty Images
48 (*left to right*) Courtesy of Rollerblade Inc.; courtesy of Yamaha Motor Corporation U.S.A.; courtesy of Long Island Savings Bank; courtesy of Sears Roebuck and Co.; courtesy of Kawasaki Motors Corp. U.S.A.
51 (*left to right*) © age Fotostock; © Jonathan Kirn/Getty Images; © Laurence Monneret/Getty Images
52 (*top*) © Ary Diesendruck/Getty Images; (*middle, left to right*) © Robert Frerck/Getty Images; © Martha Cooper/Viesti Associates; (*bottom*) © Henry Westheim
53 © Satoru Ohmori/Getty Images
55 (*top to bottom*) © Robert Frerck/Odyssey Productions/Chicago; courtesy of Korean Cultural Service; © AP/Wide World Photos

56 © Judith Collins/Alamy
57 © Paul Chesly/Getty Images
58 (*left to right*) © Austrian Archives/Corbis; © National Motor Museum/Motoring Picture Library/Alamy; © Ford Motor Co./AP/Wide World Photos
59 © Rick Gomez/Masterfile
63 © Ed Taylor Studio/Getty Images
65 © Gabe Palmer/Corbis
67 (*left to right*) © PBNJ Productions/Corbis; © George Shelley/Masterfile; © Larry Williams/Corbis
69 © Stewart Cohen/Getty Images
71 (*left to right*) © Syracuse Newspapers/Brian Phillips/The Image Works; © Tom Rosenthal/SuperStock; © Jeffrey Zaruba/Getty Images
72 © Peter Bennett/Ambient Images Inc./Alamy
73 (*left to right*) © Fotosearch; © George Kerrigan; © Amblin/Universal/The Kobal Collection; © George Kerrigan; © Robbie Jack/Corbis
74 (*left to right*) © Fergus O'Brien/Getty Images; © Dennis Hallinan/Getty Images; © Bob Higbee/Getty Images
76 (*top to bottom*) © Robert Frerck/Getty Images; © Sebastian Goll/Alamy; © Steve Raymer/Corbis
77 (*left to right*) © LifeinAsia.com; © Carl & Ann Purcell/Corbis; courtesy of the Stollwerk Museum
78 (*left to right*) © Neal Preston/Corbis; © Carlo Allegri/Getty Images; © Reuters/Corbis
80 © Juliet Coombe/Lonely Planet
83 (*left to right*) © ITAR-TASS/Yuri Belinsky/Newscom; © Mobile Press Register/Corbis; courtesy of Alexandra Nechita
84 © Warner Brothers/courtesy of Everett Collection
86 (*clockwise from top left*) © 20th Century Fox Film Corp./Everett Collection; © New Line/courtesy of Everett Collection; © Rufus F. Folkks/Corbis; © Columbia Pictures/courtesy of Everett Collection
87 © Damian Dovarganes/AP/Wide World Photos
89 © Universal/Marvel Entertainment/The Kobal Collection
90 © Fat Free Ltd./Miramax/The Kobal Collection/David Appleby
91 (*left to right*) © Reuters/Corbis; © George Kerrigan
105 © Ariel Skelly/Corbis
IA2 (*clockwise from top left*) © Corbis; © Tibor Bognar/Corbis; © age Fotostock; © James Marshall/Corbis
IA5A © Richard Price/Getty Images
IA5B © Liysa King/Getty Images
IA8 (*left to right*) © Corbis; © David Ball/Corbis; © Chuck Savage/Corbis
SS4 © George Kerrigan
SS11 © Getty Images
SS13 © George Kerrigan